THE STUDENTS' J.B.

THE GOSPEL
ACCORDING TO
SAINT JOHN

THE STUDENTS' J.B.

THE GOSPEL ACCORDING TO SAINT JOHN

With notes and commentary
by
K. S. L. Clark
B.A.Oxon.

LONDON
DARTON, LONGMAN & TODD

First published in Great Britain in 1978 by
Darton, Longman & Todd Limited
89 Lillie Road, London SW6 1UD

Jerusalem Bible text and notes © 1966, 1967 and 1968
by Darton, Longman & Todd Ltd
and Doubleday & Company Inc.
Students' notes and commentary © 1978 by K. S. L. Clark

Printed in Great Britain by
Western Printing Services Ltd, Bristol
and bound by William Brendon & Son Ltd
of Tiptree, Essex

ISBN 0 232 51400 3

INTRODUCTION

A. *The Tradition*

According to tradition the Fourth Gospel, three New Testament letters, and the Book of Revelation were all written by John the Apostle, brother of James and son of Zebedee, called by Jesus at the beginning of his ministry (Mk 1:16–20). The tradition is based on early documents. Polycarp, a bishop of Smyrna in Asia Minor and martyred in 155, had amongst his students a man named Irenaeus who later became famous as a bishop and scholar. In his book *Against Heresies*, Irenaeus recalled the reminiscences of his old teacher and what they had meant to him. Polycarp had loved to tell how he had known John 'the disciple of the Lord', and of conversations with him and others who had seen Jesus. Irenaeus said that John wrote his gospel after the others, and identified him with 'the disciple Jesus loved', only mentioned as such in the Fourth Gospel and in stories which have no parallel in the other three. He said also that John was still living, a very old man, in the reign of Trajan (98–117). A letter to the pope from the bishop of Ephesus contemporary with Irenaeus substantiates these statements and adds that John was buried at Ephesus. If John was seventeen or eighteen when he was called about the year 30, he would have been nearly ninety by the turn of the century.

The tradition is very important but at the same time it presents grave difficulties. Some of these have to do with the documents already mentioned and are too complex to go into here, but there are others which the general reader can easily appreciate. John, the son of Zebedee the Galilean fisherman, would have had a minimal education, exclusively scriptural in content, at the local synagogue. The Fourth Gospel, as it is often called, is a subtle work of great literary skill. Written in Greek like the rest of the New Testament, it is much more polished in language and style than Mark's gospel and has none of the scribal characteristics of Matthew's; it is a question whether John the Apostle could have broken so completely from the mould of his youth and produced a work of this kind. Though the author was almost certainly a Jew, he does not show the familiarity with Palestine and the conflicting parties evident in the synoptic gospels. One is bound to ask too if the writer would have described himself as 'the disciple Jesus loved', or if he would have thought it savoured of presumption to do so. The connection of John with Ephesus poses a problem of a different kind. The Acts of the Apostles and St Paul's letters together provide a clear picture of the spread of the Church from its starting point in Jerusalem to most of the major cities of the Roman Empire, but after the early chapters in Acts John's name is never mentioned. Neither in the vivid account of St Paul's mission at Ephesus and farewell to the elders there (Acts 18:24–19:41; 20:18–38) nor in the letter to the Ephesians is there any reference to him. It is possible of course that John went to Ephesus after the early sixties when the letter to the Ephesians was probably written, but according to the tradition he took Mary the mother of Jesus there after the crucifixion (Jn 19:26), and it is there that she is said to have died. Their home would have been the centre of the Christian community there.

The problem of the authorship of the Fourth Gospel may never be solved but there is no doubt that it was written towards the close of the first century. A fragment dating from the first decade of the second century has been found, and allowing time for it to have become known and valued, it would most probably have been written between 90 and 100. It was accepted as authoritative at a very early stage.

B. *The Author's Environment*

Any original work necessarily reflects the background against which it has been produced. Some knowledge therefore of the society, culture, and intellectual life in the Roman Empire at the beginning of the second century helps towards an understanding of the Fourth Gospel.

(1) The Greek language, philosophy, religion, and way of life were introduced into the Middle East by Alexander the Great in the fourth century B.C. It was a deliberate policy which was continued by the generals who divided the empire among themselves after his death. The result was a fusion of Asiatic cultures established in the region through centuries of conquest by successive Asiatic powers—Assyria, Babylon, and Persia—with a Greek culture which had lost the originality and brilliance of its flowering in the fifth century B.C. This blend of Asiatic and Greek culture is known as Hellenism ('hellene' = Greek). When the whole region including Greece itself was conquered by the Romans, they assimilated the culture of their conquered peoples and adopted the Greek language as well. Greek thus became the common language of a multi-racial society and it was for that reason that the documents eventually collected to form the New Testament were written in Greek.

(2) For any Jew, the war against the Romans (66–70) which ended in the destruction of Jerusalem and the obliteration of the Jewish nation was a catastrophic event, but for gentiles the first century was a time of peace and considerable prosperity. Roman legions effectively protected the frontiers from barbarian inroads and maintained internal security; trade flourished, travel was remarkably safe, and many enjoyed a high standard of living with leisure to read, think, and debate.

(3) There was a common search for a satisfactory explanation for the existence of the universe and the phenomenon of man within it. People believed themselves to be at the mercy of malevolent spirits and inexorable fate, and longed for an assurance of immortality. The ancient gods of Asia, Greece, and Rome were still worshipped but were losing much of their popularity amongst the thoughtful because of their crudity and the excesses of the various cults. Only one form of worship was obligatory, the worship of the emperor. It was a valuable test of the loyalty of many subject peoples. Only the Jewish communities established in most of the large cities were exempt; it was accepted that nothing would break their refusal to conform and as citizens they were too valuable to lose.

(4) Many gentiles found in Judaism an answer to their problems. They accepted the moral discipline demanded by the synagogue authorities and were then allowed to join in synagogue worship as learners or God-fearers as they were called. Cornelius the centurion (Acts 10) was a man of this kind. Only by accepting circumcision could they be received as Jews by the community.

(5) Philosophy suggested other ways of considering man's predicament. John's familiarity with this enabled him to convey his message in language which intel-

lectuals were used to and to correct erroneous ideas. Jews as well as gentiles were often conversant with Greek modes of thought but it is a question whether Zebedee's son could in adult life have come to use them with such facility. Plato taught of a transcendent God, far above and removed from creation; John emphasises the fact that God is Father closely concerned with man, and to be seen in Jesus (14:9). Plato taught of an invisible and perfect world above of which this material and imperfect world is a copy; John uses this conception in the Platonic manner whereas Jews normally contrasted the present world with the world to come, at the end of time (8:23; 18:36). The description of Jesus as the 'true' bread (6:35) and the 'true' vine (15:1) is an example of the same idea; we are to understand that Jesus is the heavenly reality brought within human perspective. The opening sentence of the gospel is a supreme instance of John's capacity to use thought-forms of equal significance but different in meaning to Jews and gentiles, to lead them to a Christian conclusion. 'In the beginning', he says, 'was the Word', in Greek the Logos. Gentiles would take this as a reference to Reason, said by the Stoic philosophers to be the divine and innermost substance of everything including man, and existing before the material world came into being. The Jews would find the language equally familiar but would put a different interpretation on the words which will be explained in the notes on the text. But both gentiles and Jews would share a common understanding when they were told that the 'Word was made flesh' (1:14).

(6) A variety of cults known as mystery religions formed an important element in the religious life of the first century. It was hoped that by the acquisition of

secret knowledge it would be possible to escape from the domination of evil powers and attain salvation and access to the presence of some mythical personage. After initiation ceremonies which required great courage and endurance, the devotee was allowed to participate in sacramental rites which made him semi-divine. Success in the enterprise depended entirely on the individual himself, his perseverance and natural endowments. John seems to have known about the activities of these cults and understood the aspirations of which they were the expression. He teaches that the knowledge to be sought is no secret available only to a few, but knowledge of a person; the dynamic experience of the living Christ. Here is no legendary figure but a historical person who having died on the cross was raised from the dead to open the way of salvation to all mankind. The true sacraments are not magical rites depending for their efficacy on the strenuous efforts of the participant, but the God-given means whereby the faithful are enabled to grow in obedience, sustained by his own life.

C. *The Fourth Gospel and the Synoptic Gospels*

The first three gospels have much material in common in addition to the Passion Narrative (the story of Christ's suffering, death, and resurrection), the core of the Good News, the one Gospel of which we have four versions. Because of their similarity Mt, Mk, and Lk are often called the synoptic gospels (synoptic = seen from the same point of view). It is impossible to say for certain what knowledge John had of them but it is generally supposed that he knew Mk, and the source peculiar to Lk though not the whole gospel of Lk as we know it.

Jn's differences from the synoptics can sometimes be explained on theological grounds and sometimes no doubt they derive from traditions not available to the synoptists. It will be convenient to list here some of the major differences in Jn but there will be further reference to them in the notes on the text. In Jn two passovers are mentioned in addition to the final one when Jesus was crucified; the scene of the ministry is for the most part in Judaea and not Galilee; the cleansing of the Temple is placed at the beginning of the ministry not at the close; the crucifixion is dated clearly and significantly in the hours immediately preceding the passover, a point which is obscure in the other gospels. Of the synoptic miracle stories only the miracle of the loaves has a place in Jn though there are resemblances in three others (4:46–54; 5:2–9; 9:1–7). Finally, the teaching in Jn is in the form of long discourses very different from the vivid parables and pithy sayings preserved in the synoptics. The rabbis used a variety of techniques and it is fair to suppose that Jesus did too. A passage in Mt strongly reminiscent of Jn (Mt 11:25–30) suggests that the discourses can be accepted as typical of one of his methods.

D. *The Purpose and Structure of the Gospel*

John's purpose was neither to supplement nor correct the earlier gospels and therefore we do not have to decide in favour of any as being the most accurate. John's object was to produce a lesson book which would be intelligible to Jews and gentiles alike, and with that purpose in view he chose and arranged his material with great deliberation.

The story of Christ's ministry is fitted into the framework of three successive passovers. For John we can be

11

certain that the primary importance of this was theological as will shortly be explained, but for us the fact
that there were three is of great historical interest
because a definite length for the ministry is indicated, a
point about which the synoptists are imprecise. Three
lesser feasts—one unspecified, the feast of Tabernacles,
and the feast of Dedication—emphasise John's main
purpose. Two great acts of salvation are being contrasted: God's deliverance of Israel from slavery in
Egypt of which the passover is the annual commemoration, and Christ's much mightier salvation of the
whole world from the slavery of sin through his death
upon the cross and resurrection, of which every
Eucharist is a commemoration. As the latter act far
surpasses the former, so do the benefits which Christ
bestows far exceed those available in Judaism. Christ
himself is the Gospel, the Good News, and he has to be
seen and known through what he did. Out of a great
mass of material therefore (19:30), John selected six
miracles as illustrating fundamental aspects of Christ's
nature and work, for that reason calling them 'signs';
the seventh and supreme sign is the death and resurrection of Jesus, and his gift of the Holy Spirit. The
account of the third, fourth, and fifth signs is followed
by discussion and teaching, and lengthy instruction
(chs 14–17) is given in preparation for the seventh. It is
important to be on the alert throughout the gospel for
double or even triple implications; what Jesus did
during his earthly ministry he continues to effect in the
daily experience of the post-resurrection Church while
all the time he reigns in heaven, 'with God in the
beginning' (1:2).

E. *The Miracles*

The miracles of Jesus are part of the original tradition about him and if we believe that he was indeed the Son of God, it is only logical to suppose that he did them. They do not prove his divinity (ordinary people have sometimes been gifted with miraculous power); only the resurrection, the ultimate and unique miracle, makes us sure of that, and the existence of the Church is inexplicable unless it really happened. All four evangelists accepted the miracles of Jesus as visual aids to the understanding of what he continues to do in the inner life of individuals. The actuality of the forgiveness of sin with its release from the crippling sense of guilt is to be learnt from the restoration to health of the bedridden man (Mk 2:1–12); it was possible for him to shoulder a burden again and work. The restoration of sight represents the gift of spiritual insight to recognise Jesus for who he is (Jn 9:1–41). Of the six miracles in Jn, three fall into this category; the miracle of the loaves, common to all four gospels, has its own distinctive significance, explained in the discourse following the account of it in ch. 6.

The two remaining miracles in Jn, the turning of the water into wine at Cana (2:1–11) and the raising of Lazarus (11:17–44), often pose a problem for the general reader. They seem inconsistent with the synoptic emphasis on the refusal of Jesus to force belief (Mt 4:5–6), and his frequent instructions to people he had cured to keep the matter secret; they also challenge credulity in a way that the healing miracles do not. We can believe that Jesus had the power to turn the water into wine but are driven to wonder if he would have provided a village wedding party with such a super-abundance, something like a hundred and eighty gallons. The raising of Lazarus from the dead is marvel enough but the fact that he had been dead three days makes it a demonstration of power which seems out of all proportion in the context in which it was exercised; the two sisters loved their brother and no doubt depended on him but there is nothing in the story to suggest that their lives would go to pieces without him, and death is something we all have to adjust to. John himself no doubt believed that the events took place as described (19:34; 20:30–31; 21:34). However, his sole preoccupation, we can be sure, was not with the stupendous nature of the events as such, but with the vital truths about Jesus which they suggest; they were signs of enduring truth which nearly two thousand years of Christian experience can vouch for.

INTERPRETATION OF THE TEXT

The following works have been consulted:
The Gospel according to St John by C. K. Barrett
The Gospel of St John by John Marsh
St John's Gospel by R. H. Lightfoot
The Gospel of John by G. H. C. MacGregor
The Jerusalem Bible, Standard Edition

THE GOSPEL
ACCORDING TO
SAINT JOHN

Note. In this Gospel, the text is printed in paragraphs and not as a succession of separate units called verses. In case any comparison with other versions is necessary, the verse-numbers (as used in the Vulgate, Authorised Version, etc.) are printed in the margin and a dot (·) shows where the numbered verse begins, if this is in the middle of a line. (If a verse-number is missing, this is because the Jerusalem Bible follows a text that differs from that followed by the older translations.)

Italic type indicates an identifiable quotation, normally from a book of the Old Testament.

PROLOGUE

1 **1** In the beginning was the Word:
the Word was with God
and the Word was God.

2 He was with God in the beginning.

3 Through him all things came to be,
not one thing had its being but through him.

4 All that came to be had life in him
and that life was the light of men,

5 a light that shines in the dark,
a light that darkness could not overpower.[a]

6 A man came, sent by God.
His name was John.

7 He came as a witness,
as a witness to speak for the light,
so that everyone might believe through him.

8 He was not the light,
only a witness to speak for the light.

9 The Word was the true light
that enlightens all men;
and he was coming into the world.

10 He was in the world
that had its being through him,
and the world did not know him.

11 He came to his own domain
and his own people did not accept him.

12 But to all who did accept him

1 a. Or 'grasp', in the sense of 'enclose' or 'understand'.

19

he gave power to become children of God,
to all who believe in the name of him
who was born not out of human stock   13
or urge of the flesh
or will of man
but of God himself.
The Word was made flesh,   14
he lived among us,[b]
and we saw his glory,
the glory that is his as the only Son of the Father,
full of grace and truth.

John appears as his witness. He proclaims: 15
'This is the one of whom I said:
He who comes after me
ranks before me
because he existed before me'.

Indeed, from his fulness we have, all of us,   16
    received—
yes, grace in return for grace,
since, though the Law was given through Moses,   17
grace and truth have come through Jesus Christ.
No one has ever seen God;   18
it is the only Son, who is nearest to the Father's
    heart,
who has made him known.

I. THE FIRST PASSOVER

A. THE OPENING WEEK

The witness of John

This is how John appeared as a witness. When the 19
Jews[c] sent priests and Levites from Jerusalem to ask

20 him, 'Who are you?' ·he not only declared, but he
21 declared quite openly, 'I am not the Christ'. ·'Well
then,' they asked 'are you Elijah?'[d] 'I am not' he said.
22 'Are you the Prophet?'[e] He answered, 'No'. ·So they
said to him, 'Who are you? We must take back an
answer to those who sent us. What have you to say
23 about yourself?' ·So John said, 'I am, as Isaiah
prophesied:

> *a voice that cries in the wilderness:*
> *Make a straight way for the Lord'.*[f]

24
25 Now these men had been sent by the Pharisees, ·and
they put this further question to him, 'Why are you
baptising if you are not the Christ, and not Elijah, and
26 not the prophet?' ·John replied, 'I baptise with water;
27 but there stands among you—unknown to you—·the one
who is coming after me; and I am not fit to undo his
28 sandal-strap'. ·This happened at Bethany, on the far
side of the Jordan, where John was baptising.

29 The next day, seeing Jesus coming towards him,
John said, 'Look, there is the lamb of God that takes
30 away the sin of the world. ·This is the one I spoke of
when I said: A man is coming after me who ranks before
31 me because he existed before me. ·I did not know him
myself, and yet it was to reveal him to Israel that I came
32 baptising with water.' ·John also declared, 'I saw the
Spirit coming down on him from heaven like a dove
33 and resting on him. ·I did not know him myself, but he
who sent me to baptise with water had said to me,
"The man on whom you see the Spirit come down and

b. 'pitched his tent among us'.   **c.** In Jn this usually indicates the
Jewish religious authorities who were hostile to Jesus; but occasionally
the Jews as a whole.   **d.** Whose return was expected, Ml 3:23-24.
e. The Prophet greater than Moses who was expected as Messiah, on
an interpretation of Dt 18:15.   **f.** Is 40:3.

rest is the one who is going to baptise with the Holy Spirit". ·Yes, I have seen and I am the witness that he 34 is the Chosen One of God.'

The first disciples

On the following day as John stood there again with 35 two of his disciples, ·Jesus passed, and John stared hard 36 at him and said, 'Look, there is the lamb of God'. Hearing this, the two disciples followed Jesus. ·Jesus 37 turned round, saw them following and said, 'What do 38 you want?' They answered, 'Rabbi,'—which means Teacher—'where do you live?' ·'Come and see' he 39 replied; so they went and saw where he lived, and stayed with him the rest of that day. It was about the tenth hour.[g]

One of these two who became followers of Jesus after 40 hearing what John had said was Andrew, the brother of Simon Peter. ·Early next morning, Andrew met his 41 brother and said to him, 'We have found the Messiah'— which means the Christ—·and he took Simon to Jesus. 42 Jesus looked hard at him and said, 'You are Simon son of John; you are to be called Cephas'—meaning Rock.

The next day, after Jesus had decided to leave for 43 Galilee, he met Philip and said, 'Follow me'. ·Philip 44 came from the same town, Bethsaida, as Andrew and Peter. ·Philip found Nathanael[h] and said to him, 'We 45 have found the one Moses wrote about in the Law, the one about whom the prophets wrote: he is Jesus son of Joseph, from Nazareth'. ·'From Nazareth?' said 46 Nathanael, 'Can anything good come from that place?' 'Come and see' replied Philip. ·When Jesus saw 47 Nathanael coming he said of him, 'There is an Israelite who deserves the name, incapable of deceit'. ·'How do 48 you know me?' said Nathanael. 'Before Philip came to

call you,' said Jesus 'I saw you under the fig tree.'
49 Nathanael answered, 'Rabbi, you are the Son of God,
50 you are the King of Israel'. ·Jesus replied, 'You believe
that just because I said: I saw you under the fig tree.
51 You will see greater things than that.' ·And then he
added, 'I tell you most solemnly, you will see heaven
laid open and, above the Son of Man, the angels of God
ascending and descending'.

The wedding at Cana

1 2 Three days later there was a wedding at Cana in
2 Galilee. The mother of Jesus was there, ·and Jesus
3 and his disciples had also been invited. ·When they ran
out of wine, since the wine provided for the wedding
was all finished, the mother of Jesus said to him, 'They
4 have no wine'. ·Jesus said, 'Woman, why turn to me?
5 My hour has not come yet.' ·His mother said to the
6 servants, ·'*Do whatever he tells you*'.*a* ·There were six
stone water jars standing there, meant for the ablutions
that are customary among the Jews: each could hold
7 twenty or thirty gallons. ·Jesus said to the servants,
'Fill the jars with water', and they filled them to the
8 brim. ·'Draw some out now' he told them 'and take it
9 to the steward.' ·They did this; the steward tasted the
water, and it had turned into wine. Having no idea
where it came from—only the servants who had drawn
the water knew—the steward called the bridegroom
10 and said, 'People generally serve the best wine first,
and keep the cheaper sort till the guests have had plenty
to drink; but you have kept the best wine till now'.
11 This was the first of the signs given by Jesus: it was
given at Cana in Galilee. He let his glory be seen, and

g. 4 p.m.   h. Probably the Bartholomew of the other gospels.
2 a. Gn 41:55.

his disciples believed in him. ·After this he went down 12
to Capernaum with his mother and the brothers, but
they stayed there only a few days.

B. THE PASSOVER

The cleansing of the Temple

Just before the Jewish Passover Jesus went up to 13
Jerusalem, ·and in the Temple he found people selling 14
cattle and sheep and pigeons, and the money changers
sitting at their counters there. ·Making a whip out of 15
some cord, he drove them all out of the Temple, cattle
and sheep as well, scattered the money changers' coins,
knocked their tables over ·and said to the pigeon- 16
sellers, 'Take all this out of here and stop turning my
Father's house into a market'. ·Then his disciples 17
remembered the words of scripture: *Zeal for your house
will devour me.*[b] ·The Jews intervened and said, 'What 18
sign can you show us to justify what you have done?'
Jesus answered, 'Destroy this sanctuary, and in three 19
days I will raise it up'. ·The Jews replied, 'It has taken 20
forty-six years to build this sanctuary:[c] are you going
to raise it up in three days?' ·But he was speaking of 21
the sanctuary that was his body, ·and when Jesus rose 22
from the dead, his disciples remembered that he had
said this, and they believed the scripture and the words
he had said.

During his stay in Jerusalem for the Passover many 23
believed in his name when they saw the signs that he
gave, ·but Jesus knew them all and did not trust himself 24
to them; ·he never needed evidence about any man; he 25
could tell what a man had in him.

C. THE MYSTERY OF THE SPIRIT REVEALED TO A MASTER IN ISRAEL

The conversation with Nicodemus

1 2 **3** There was one of the Pharisees called Nicodemus, a leading Jew, ·who came to Jesus by night and said, 'Rabbi, we know that you are a teacher who comes from God; for no one could perform the signs that you 3 do unless God were with him'. ·Jesus answered:

> 'I tell you most solemnly,
> unless a man is born from above,
> he cannot see the kingdom of God'.

4 Nicodemus said, 'How can a grown man be born? Can he go back into his mother's womb and be born 5 again?' ·Jesus replied:

> 'I tell you most solemnly,
> unless a man is born through water and the
>   Spirit,
> he cannot enter the kingdom of God:
6 > what is born of the flesh is flesh;
> what is born of the Spirit is spirit.
7 > Do not be surprised when I say:
> You must be born from above.
8 > The wind blows wherever it pleases;
> you hear its sound,
> but you cannot tell where it comes from or where
>   it is going.
> That is how it is with all who are born of the
>   Spirit.'

b. Ps 69:9.   **c.** Reconstruction work on the Temple began in 19 B.C. This is therefore the Passover of 28 A.D.

'How can that be possible?' asked Nicodemus. ·'You, 9
a teacher in Israel, and you do not know these things!' 10
replied Jesus.

'I tell you most solemnly,   11
we speak only about what we know
and witness only to what we have seen
and yet you people reject our evidence.
If you do not believe me   12
when I speak about things in this world,
how are you going to believe me
when I speak to you about heavenly things?
No one has gone up to heaven   13
except the one who came down from heaven,
the Son of Man who is in heaven;
and the Son of Man must be lifted up
as Moses lifted up the serpent in the desert,   14
so that everyone who believes may have eternal   15
    life in him.
Yes, God loved the world so much   16
that he gave his only Son,
so that everyone who believes in him may not
    be lost
but may have eternal life.
For God sent his Son into the world   17
not to condemn the world,
but so that through him the world might be
    saved.
No one who believes in him will be condemned;   18
but whoever refuses to believe is condemned
    already,
because he has refused to believe
in the name of God's only Son.
On these grounds is sentence pronounced: 19

26

that though the light has come into the world
men have shown they prefer
darkness to the light
because their deeds were evil.
20 And indeed, everybody who does wrong
hates the light and avoids it,
for fear his actions should be exposed;
21 but the man who lives by the truth
comes out into the light,
so that it may be plainly seen that what he does
is done in God.'

II. JOURNEYS IN SAMARIA AND GALILEE

John bears witness for the last time

22 After this, Jesus went with his disciples into the Judaean countryside and stayed with them there and 23 baptised. ·At the same time John was baptising at Aenon[a] near Salim, where there was plenty of water, 24 and people were going there to be baptised. ·This was before John had been put in prison.

25 Now some of John's disciples had opened a discus-26 sion with a Jew about purification, ·so they went to John and said, 'Rabbi, the man who was with you on the far side of the Jordan, the man to whom you bore witness, is baptising now; and everyone is going to 27 him'. ·John replied:

'A man can lay claim
only to what is given him from heaven.

3 a. A tradition locates Aenon ('Springs') in the Jordan valley 7 m. from Scythopolis.

'You yourselves can bear me out: I said: I myself am 28
not the Christ; I am the one who has been sent in front
of him.

'The bride is only for the bridegroom;   29
and yet the bridegroom's friend,
who stands there and listens,
is glad when he hears the bridegroom's voice.
This same joy I feel, and now it is complete.
He must grow greater,   30
I must grow smaller.
He who comes from above   31
is above all others;
he who is born of the earth
is earthly himself and speaks in an earthly way.
He who comes from heaven
bears witness to the things he has seen and   32
    heard,
even if his testimony is not accepted;
though all who do accept his testimony   33
are attesting the truthfulness of God,
since he whom God has sent
speaks God's own words:
God gives him the Spirit without reserve.
The Father loves the Son
and has entrusted everything to him.
Anyone who believes in the Son has eternal life,
but anyone who refuses to believe in the Son
    will never see life:
the anger of God stays on him.'

The saviour of the world revealed to the Samaritans

4 When Jesus heard that the Pharisees had found out 1
that he was making and baptising more disciples

2 than John—·though in fact it was his disciples who
3 baptised, not Jesus himself—·he left Judaea and went
4 back to Galilee. ·This meant that he had to cross
Samaria.

5   On the way he came to the Samaritan town called
Sychar,[a] near the land that Jacob gave to his son
6 Joseph. ·Jacob's well is there and Jesus, tired by the
journey, sat straight down by the well. It was about the
7 sixth hour.[b] ·When a Samaritan woman came to draw
8 water, Jesus said to her, 'Give me a drink'. ·His disciples
9 had gone into the town to buy food. ·The Samaritan
woman said to him, 'What? You are a Jew and you ask
me, a Samaritan, for a drink?'—Jews, in fact, do not
10 associate with Samaritans. ·Jesus replied:

> 'If you only knew what God is offering
> and who it is that is saying to you:
> Give me a drink,
> you would have been the one to ask,
> and he would have given you living water'.

11   'You have no bucket, sir,' she answered 'and the well
12 is deep: how could you get this living water? ·Are you
a greater man than our father Jacob who gave us this
well and drank from it himself with his sons and his
13 cattle?' ·Jesus replied:

> 'Whoever drinks this water
> will get thirsty again;
14   but anyone who drinks the water that I shall give
> will never be thirsty again:
> the water that I shall give
> will turn into a spring inside him, welling up to
>   eternal life'.

4 a. Either Shechem (Aramaic: Sichara), or Askar at the foot of Mt
Ebal. 'Jacob's Well' is not mentioned in Gn.   **b.** Noon.

'Sir,' said the woman 'give me some of that water, so 15
that I may never get thirsty and never have to come
here again to draw water.' ·'Go and call your husband' 16
said Jesus to her 'and come back here.' ·The woman 17
answered, 'I have no husband'. He said to her, 'You
are right to say, "I have no husband"; ·for although 18
you have had five, the one you have now is not your
husband. You spoke the truth there.' ·'I see you are a 19
prophet, sir' said the woman. ·'Our fathers worshipped 20
on this mountain,*c* while you say that Jerusalem is the
place where one ought to worship.' ·Jesus said: 21

'Believe me, woman, the hour is coming
when you will worship the Father
neither on this mountain nor in Jerusalem.
You worship what you do not know;   22
we worship what we do know;
for salvation comes from the Jews.
But the hour will come—in fact it is here already— 23
when true worshippers will worship the Father
        in spirit and truth:
that is the kind of worshipper
the Father wants.
God is spirit,   24
and those who worship
must worship in spirit and truth.'

The woman said to him, 'I know that Messiah—that 25
is, Christ—is coming; and when he comes he will tell us
everything'. ·'I who am speaking to you,' said Jesus 'I 26
am he.'

At this point his disciples returned, and were sur- 27
prised to find him speaking to a woman, though none
of them asked, 'What do you want from her?' or, 'Why
are you talking to her?' ·The woman put down her 28

water jar and hurried back to the town to tell the people,
29 'Come and see a man who has told me everything I
30 ever did; I wonder if he is the Christ?' ·This brought
people out of the town and they started walking
towards him.

31 Meanwhile, the disciples were urging him, 'Rabbi,
32 do have something to eat'; ·but he said, 'I have food
33 to eat that you do not know about'. ·So the disciples
asked one another, 'Has someone been bringing him
34 food?' ·But Jesus said:

> 'My food
> is to do the will of the one who sent me,
> and to complete his work.
> 35   Have you not got a saying:
> Four months and then the harvest?
> Well, I tell you:
> Look around you, look at the fields;
> already they are white, ready for harvest!
> 36   Already ·the reaper is being paid his wages,
> already he is bringing in the grain for eternal life,
> and thus sower and reaper rejoice together.
> 37   For here the proverb holds good:
> one sows, another reaps;
> 38   I sent you to reap
> a harvest you had not worked for.
> Others worked for it;
> and you have come into the rewards of their
>   trouble.'

39 Many Samaritans of that town had believed in him
on the strength of the woman's testimony when she
40 said, 'He told me all I have ever done', ·so, when the

---

c. Gerizim, the mountain on which the Samaritans built a rival to the
Jerusalem Temple: it was destroyed by Hyrcanus, 129 B.C.

Samaritans came up to him, they begged him to stay with them. He stayed for two days, and ·when he spoke 41 to them many more came to believe; ·and they said to 42 the woman, 'Now we no longer believe because of what you told us; we have heard him ourselves and we know that he really is the saviour of the world'.

The cure of the nobleman's son

When the two days were over Jesus left for Galilee. 43 He himself had declared that there is no respect for a 44 prophet in his own country, ·but on his arrival the 45 Galileans received him well, having seen all that he had done at Jerusalem during the festival which they too had attended.

He went again to Cana in Galilee, where he had 46 changed the water into wine. Now there was a court official there whose son was ill at Capernaum ·and, 47 hearing that Jesus had arrived in Galilee from Judaea, he went and asked him to come and cure his son as he was at the point of death. ·Jesus said, 'So you will not 48 believe unless you see signs and portents!' ·'Sir,' 49 answered the official 'come down before my child dies.' 'Go home,' said Jesus 'your son will live.' The man 50 believed what Jesus had said and started on his way; and while he was still on the journey back his servants 51 met him with the news that his boy was alive. ·He asked 52 them when the boy had begun to recover. 'The fever left him yesterday' they said 'at the seventh hour.' ·The 53 father realised that this was exactly the time when Jesus had said, 'Your son will live'; and he and all his household believed.

This was the second sign given by Jesus, on his return 54 from Judaea to Galilee.

III. THE SECOND FEAST AT JERUSALEM

The cure of a sick man at the Pool of Bethzatha

1 5 Some time after this there was a Jewish festival, and
2 Jesus went up to Jerusalem. ·Now at the Sheep Pool
in Jerusalem there is a building, called Bethzatha in
3 Hebrew, consisting of five porticos; ·and under these
were crowds of sick people—blind, lame, paralysed—
4 waiting for the water to move; ·for at intervals the
angel of the Lord came down into the pool, and the
water was disturbed, and the first person to enter the
water after this disturbance was cured of any ailment
5 he suffered from. ·One man there had an illness which
6 had lasted thirty-eight years, ·and when Jesus saw him
lying there and knew he had been in this condition for
a long time, he said, 'Do you want to be well again?'
7 'Sir,' replied the sick man 'I have no one to put me into
the pool when the water is disturbed; and while I am
still on the way, someone else gets there before me.'
8 Jesus said, 'Get up, pick up your sleeping-mat and
9 walk'. ·The man was cured at once, and he picked up
his mat and walked away.

10 Now that day happened to be the sabbath, ·so the
Jews said to the man who had been cured, 'It is the
sabbath; you are not allowed to carry your sleeping-
11 mat'. ·He replied, 'But the man who cured me told me,
12 "Pick up your mat and walk" '. ·They asked, 'Who is
the man who said to you, "Pick up your mat and
13 walk"?' ·The man had no idea who it was, since Jesus
had disappeared into the crowd that filled the place.
14 After a while Jesus met him in the Temple and said,

B 33

'Now you are well again, be sure not to sin any more, or something worse may happen to you'. ·The man went 15 back and told the Jews that it was Jesus who had cured him. ·It was because he did things like this on the 16 sabbath that the Jews began to persecute Jesus. ·His 17 answer to them was, 'My Father goes on working, and so do I'. ·But that only made the Jews even more intent 18 on killing him, because, not content with breaking the sabbath, he spoke of God as his own Father, and so made himself God's equal.

To this accusation Jesus replied: 19

'I tell you most solemnly,
the Son can do nothing by himself;
he can do only what he sees the Father doing:
and whatever the Father does the Son does too.
For the Father loves the Son   20
and shows him everything he does himself,
and he will show him even greater things than
        these,
works that will astonish you.
Thus, as the Father raises the dead and gives   21
        them life,
so the Son gives life to anyone he chooses;
for the Father judges no one;   22
he has entrusted all judgement to the Son,
so that all may honour the Son   23
as they honour the Father.
Whoever refuses honour to the Son
refuses honour to the Father who sent him.
I tell you most solemnly,   24
whoever listens to my words,
and believes in the one who sent me,
has eternal life;

34

without being brought to judgement
he has passed from death to life.

25 I tell you most solemnly,
the hour will come—in fact it is here already—
when the dead will hear the voice of the Son
      of God,
and all who hear it will live.

26 For the Father, who is the source of life,
has made the Son the source of life;

27 and, because he is the Son of Man,
has appointed him supreme judge.

28 Do not be surprised at this,
for the hour is coming
when the dead will leave their graves
at the sound of his voice:

29 those who did good
will rise again to life;
and those who did evil, to condemnation.

30 I can do nothing by myself;
I can only judge as I am told to judge,
and my judging is just,
because my aim is to do not my own will,
but the will of him who sent me.

31 'Were I to testify on my own behalf,
my testimony would not be valid;

32 but there is another witness who can speak on
      my behalf,
and I know that his testimony is valid.

33 You sent messengers to John,
and he gave his testimony to the truth:

34 not that I depend on human testimony;
no, it is for your salvation that I speak of this.

35 John was a lamp alight and shining

and for a time you were content to enjoy the
    light that he gave.
But my testimony is greater than John's: 36
the works my Father has given me to carry out,
these same works of mine
testify that the Father has sent me.
Besides, the Father who sent me   37
bears witness to me himself.
You have never heard his voice,
you have never seen his shape,
and his word finds no home in you   38
because you do not believe
in the one he has sent.

'You study the scriptures,   39
believing that in them you have eternal life;
now these same scriptures testify to me,
and yet you refuse to come to me for life!   40
As for human approval, this means nothing to   41
    me.
Besides, I know you too well: 42
you have no love of God in you.
I have come in the name of my Father   43
and you refuse to accept me;
if someone else comes in his own name
you will accept him.

How can you believe,   44
since you look to one another for approval
and are not concerned
with the approval that comes from the one God?
Do not imagine that I am going to accuse you   45
    before the Father:
you place your hopes on Moses,
and Moses will be your accuser.

46   If you really believed him
        you would believe me too,
        since it was I that he was writing about;
47   but if you refuse to believe what he wrote,
        how can you believe what I say?'

IV. ANOTHER PASSOVER, THE BREAD OF LIFE

The miracle of the loaves

1,2 **6** Some time after this, Jesus went off to the other side of the Sea of Galilee—or of Tiberias—·and a large crowd followed him, impressed by the signs he gave by 3 curing the sick. ·Jesus climbed the hillside, and sat down 4 there with his disciples. ·It was shortly before the Jewish feast of Passover.

5   Looking up, Jesus saw the crowds approaching and said to Philip, 'Where can we buy some bread for these 6 people to eat?' ·He only said this to test Philip; he 7 himself knew exactly what he was going to do. ·Philip answered, 'Two hundred denarii would only buy enough 8 to give them a small piece each'. ·One of his disciples, 9 Andrew, Simon Peter's brother, said, ·'There is a small boy here with five barley loaves and two fish; but what 10 is that between so many?' ·Jesus said to them, 'Make the people sit down'. There was plenty of grass there, 11 and as many as five thousand men sat down. ·Then Jesus took the loaves, gave thanks, and gave them out to all who were sitting ready; he then did the same with 12 the fish, giving out as much as was wanted. ·When they had eaten enough he said to the disciples, 'Pick up the 13 pieces left over, so that nothing gets wasted'. ·So they picked them up, and filled twelve hampers with scraps

left over from the meal of five barley loaves. ·The 14
people, seeing this sign that he had given, said, 'This
really is the prophet who is to come into the world'.
Jesus, who could see they were about to come and take 15
him by force and make him king, escaped back to the
hills by himself.

Jesus walks on the waters

That evening the disciples went down to the shore of 16
the lake and ·got into a boat to make for Capernaum 17
on the other side of the lake. It was getting dark by now
and Jesus had still not rejoined them. ·The wind was 18
strong, and the sea was getting rough. ·They had rowed 19
three or four miles when they saw Jesus walking on the
lake and coming towards the boat. This frightened
them, ·but he said, 'It is I. Do not be afraid.' ·They were 20
for taking him into the boat, but in no time it reached 21
the shore at the place they were making for.

The discourse in the synagogue at Capernaum

Next day, the crowd that had stayed on the other side 22
saw that only one boat had been there, and that Jesus
had not got into the boat with his disciples, but that the
disciples had set off by themselves. ·Other boats, how- 23
ever, had put in from Tiberias, near the place where the
bread had been eaten. ·When the people saw that neither 24
Jesus nor his disciples were there, they got into those
boats and crossed to Capernaum to look for Jesus.
When they found him on the other side, they said to 25
him, 'Rabbi, when did you come here?' ·Jesus answered: 26

'I tell you most solemnly,
you are not looking for me
because you have seen the signs

but because you had all the bread you wanted
   to eat.

27 Do not work for food that cannot last,
   but work for food that endures to eternal life,
   the kind of food the Son of Man is offering you,
   for on him the Father, God himself, has set his
      seal.'

28 Then they said to him, 'What must we do if we are
29 to do the works that God wants?' ·Jesus gave them this
answer, 'This is working for God: you must believe in
30 the one he has sent'. ·So they said, 'What sign will you
give to show us that we should believe in you? What
31 work will you do? ·Our fathers had manna to eat in
the desert; as scripture says: *He gave them bread from
heaven to eat.'*[a]

32 Jesus answered:

'I tell you most solemnly,
   it was not Moses who gave you bread from
      heaven,
   it is my Father who gives you the bread from
      heaven,
   the true bread;
33 for the bread of God
   is that which comes down from heaven
   and gives life to the world'.

34
35 'Sir,' they said 'give us that bread always.' ·Jesus
answered:

'I am the bread of life.
   He who comes to me will never be hungry;
   he who believes in me will never thirst.
36 But, as I have told you,

6 a. Ex 16:4f

you can see me and still you do not believe.
All that the Father gives me will come to me,   37
and whoever comes to me
I shall not turn him away;
because I have come from heaven,   38
not to do my own will,
but to do the will of the one who sent me.
Now the will of him who sent me   39
is that I should lose nothing
of all that he has given to me,
and that I should raise it up on the last day.
Yes, it is my Father's will   40
that whoever sees the Son and believes in him
shall have eternal life,
and that I shall raise him up on the last day.'

Meanwhile the Jews were complaining to each other 41
about him, because he had said, 'I am the bread that
came down from heaven'. ·'Surely this is Jesus son of 42
Joseph' they said. 'We know his father and mother. How
can he now say, "I have come down from heaven"?'
Jesus said in reply, 'Stop complaining to each other.   43

'No one can come to me   44
unless he is drawn by the Father who sent me,
and I will raise him up at the last day.
It is written in the prophets: 45
They will all be taught by God,[b]
and to hear the teaching of the Father,
and learn from it,
is to come to me.
Not that anybody has seen the Father,   46
except the one who comes from God:
he has seen the Father.
I tell you most solemnly,   47

everybody who believes has eternal life.
48 I am the bread of life.
49 Your fathers ate the manna in the desert
and they are dead;
50 but this is the bread that comes down from
heaven,
so that a man may eat it and not die.
51 I am the living bread which has come down
from heaven.
Anyone who eats this bread will live for ever;
and the bread that I shall give
is my flesh, for the life of the world.'

52 Then the Jews started arguing with one another:
'How can this man give us his flesh to eat?' they said.
53 Jesus replied:

'I tell you most solemnly,
if you do not eat the flesh of the Son of Man
and drink his blood,
you will not have life in you.
54 Anyone who does eat my flesh and drink my
blood
has eternal life,
and I shall raise him up on the last day.
55 For my flesh is real food
and my blood is real drink.
56 He who eats my flesh and drinks my blood
lives in me
and I live in him.
57 As I, who am sent by the living Father,
myself draw life from the Father,
so whoever eats me will draw life from me.
58 This is the bread come down from heaven;

b. Is 54:13.

not like the bread our ancestors ate:
they are dead,
but anyone who eats this bread will live for ever.'

He taught this doctrine at Capernaum, in the syna- 59
gogue. ·After hearing it, many of his followers said, 60
'This is intolerable language. How could anyone
accept it?' ·Jesus was aware that his followers were 61
complaining about it and said, 'Does this upset you? 62
What if you should see the Son of Man ascend to
where he was before?

'It is the spirit that gives life, 63
the flesh has nothing to offer.
The words I have spoken to you are spirit
and they are life.

'But there are some of you who do not believe.' For 64
Jesus knew from the outset those who did not believe,
and who it was that would betray him. ·He went on, 65
'This is why I told you that no one could come to me
unless the Father allows him'. ·After this, many of his 66
disciples left him and stopped going with him.

Peter's profession of faith

Then Jesus said to the Twelve, 'What about you, do 67
you want to go away too?' ·Simon Peter answered, 68
'Lord, who shall we go to? You have the message of
eternal life, ·and we believe; we know that you are the 69
Holy One of God.' ·Jesus replied, 'Have I not chosen 70
you, you Twelve? Yet one of you is a devil.' ·He meant 71
Judas son of Simon Iscariot, since this was the man,
one of the Twelve, who was going to betray him.

V. THE FEAST OF TABERNACLES

Jesus goes up to Jerusalem for the feast and teaches there

1 7 After this Jesus stayed in Galilee; he could not stay
in Judaea, because the Jews were out to kill him.
2
3 As the Jewish feast of Tabernacles drew near, ·his
brothers[a] said to him, 'Why not leave this place and go
to Judaea, and let your disciples[b] see the works you are
4 doing; ·if a man wants to be known he does not do
things in secret; since you are doing all this, you should
5 let the whole world see'. ·Not even his brothers, in fact,
6 had faith in him. ·Jesus answered, 'The right time for
me has not come yet, but any time is the right time for
7 you. ·The world cannot hate you, but it does hate me,
8 because I give evidence that its ways are evil. ·Go up to
the festival yourselves: I am not going to this festival,
9 because for me the time is not ripe yet.' ·Having said
that, he stayed behind in Galilee.

10 However, after his brothers had left for the festival,
he went up as well, but quite privately, without drawing
11 attention to himself. ·At the festival the Jews were on
12 the look-out for him: 'Where is he?' they said. ·People
stood in groups whispering[c] about him. Some said,
'He is a good man'; others, 'No, he is leading the
13 people astray'. ·Yet no one spoke about him openly,
for fear of the Jews.

14 When the festival was half over, Jesus went to the
15 Temple and began to teach. ·The Jews were astonished

7 a. In the wide sense, as in Mt 12:46: relations of his own generation.
b. Those in Jerusalem and Judaea.   c. Or 'In the crowds there was
whispering about him'.

and said, 'How did he learn to read? He has not been
taught.' ·Jesus answered them: 16

'My teaching is not from myself:
it comes from the one who sent me;
and if anyone is prepared to do his will, 17
he will know whether my teaching is from God
or whether my doctrine is my own.
When a man's doctrine is his own 18
he is hoping to get honour for himself;
but when he is working for the honour of one
who sent him,
then he is sincere
and by no means an impostor.
Did not Moses give you the Law? 19
And yet not one of you keeps the Law!

'Why do you want to kill me?' ·The crowd replied, 20
'You are mad! Who wants to kill you?' ·Jesus answered, 21
'One work I did, and you are all surprised by it. ·Moses 22
ordered you to practise circumcision—not that it began
with him, it goes back to the patriarchs—and you
circumcise on the sabbath. ·Now if a man can be 23
circumcised on the sabbath so that the Law of Moses is
not broken, why are you angry with me for making a
man whole and complete on a sabbath? ·Do not keep 24
judging according to appearances; let your judgement
be according to what is right.'

The people discuss the origin of the Messiah

Meanwhile some of the people of Jerusalem were 25
saying, 'Isn't this the man they want to kill? ·And here 26
he is, speaking freely, and they have nothing to say to
him! Can it be true the authorities have made up their
minds that he is the Christ? ·Yet we all know where he 27

comes from, but when the Christ appears no one will know where he comes from.'[d]

28 Then, as Jesus taught in the Temple, he cried out:

> 'Yes, you know me and you know where I came
>   from.
> Yet I have not come of myself:
> no, there is one who sent me and I really come
>   from him,
> and you do not know him,
> 29 but I know him
> because I have come from him
> and it was he who sent me.'

30 They would have arrested him then, but because his time had not yet come no one laid a hand on him.

Jesus foretells his approaching departure

31 There were many people in the crowds, however, who believed in him; they were saying, 'When the Christ comes, will he give more signs than this man?'
32 Hearing that rumours like this about him were spreading among the people, the Pharisees sent the Temple police to arrest him.
33 Then Jesus said:

> 'I shall remain with you for only a short time
>   now;
> then I shall go back to the one who sent me.
> 34 You will look for me and will not find me:
> where I am
> you cannot come.'

d. Although the prophecy that the Messiah would be born in Bethlehem was well known, it was commonly believed that he would appear suddenly from some secret place.

The Jews then said to one another, 'Where is he going 35 that we shan't be able to find him? Is he going abroad to the people who are dispersed among the Greeks and will he teach the Greeks? ·What does he mean when 36 he says:

> "You will look for me and will not find me:
> where I am,
> you cannot come"?'

The promise of living water

On the last day and greatest day of the festival, Jesus 37 stood there and cried out:

> 'If any man is thirsty, let him come to me!
> Let the man come and drink ·who believes 38
>   in me!'

As scripture says, From his breast shall flow fountains of living water.[e]

He was speaking of the Spirit which those who 39 believed in him were to receive; for there was no Spirit as yet because Jesus had not yet been glorified.

Fresh discussions on the origin of the Messiah

Several people who had been listening said, 'Surely 40 he must be the prophet', ·and some said, 'He is the 41 Christ', but others said, 'Would the Christ be from Galilee? ·Does not scripture say that the Christ must be 42 descended from David and come from the town of Bethlehem?' ·So the people could not agree about him. 43 Some would have liked to arrest him, but no one 44 actually laid hands on him.

The police went back to the chief priests and Pharisees 45 who said to them, 'Why haven't you brought him?'

46 The police replied, 'There has never been anybody
47 who has spoken like him'. ·'So' the Pharisees answered
48 'you have been led astray as well? ·Have any of the
49 authorities believed in him? Any of the Pharisees? ·This
rabble knows nothing about the Law—they are damned.'
50 One of them, Nicodemus—the same man who had come
51 to Jesus earlier—said to them, ·'But surely the Law
does not allow us to pass judgement on a man without
giving him a hearing and discovering what he is about?'
52 To this they answered, 'Are you a Galilean too? Go
into the matter, and see for yourself: prophets do not
come out of Galilee.'

The adulterous woman[f]

53
1   They all went home, **8** and Jesus went to the Mount
     of Olives.

2   At daybreak he appeared in the Temple again; and
as all the people came to him, he sat down and began
to teach them.

3   The scribes and Pharisees brought a woman along
who had been caught committing adultery; and making
4 her stand there in full view of everybody, ·they said to
Jesus, 'Master, this woman was caught in the very act
5 of committing adultery, ·and Moses has ordered us in
the Law to condemn women like this to death by
6 stoning. What have you to say?' ·They asked him this
as a test, looking for something to use against him. But
Jesus bent down and started writing on the ground with
7 his finger. ·As they persisted with their question, he

e. Life-giving water for Zion was a theme of the readings from scripture
on the feast of Tabernacles (Zc 14:8, Ezk 47:1f); the liturgy included
prayers for rain and the commemoration of the miracle of Moses and
the water, Ex 17.   f. The author of this passage is not John; the
oldest MSS do not include it or place it elsewhere. The style is that of
the Synoptics.

looked up and said, 'If there is one of you who has not sinned, let him be the first to throw a stone at her'. Then he bent down and wrote on the ground again. 8 When they heard this they went away one by one, 9 beginning with the eldest, until Jesus was left alone with the woman, who remained standing there. ·He 10 looked up and said, 'Woman, where are they? Has no one condemned you?' ·'No one, sir' she replied. 'Neither 11 do I condemn you,' said Jesus 'go away, and don't sin any more.'

Jesus, the light of the world

When Jesus spoke to the people again, he said: 12

'I am the light of the world;
anyone who follows me will not be walking in
     the dark;
he will have the light of life'.

A discussion on the testimony of Jesus to himself

At this the Pharisees said to him, 'You are testifying 13 on your own behalf; your testimony is not valid'. Jesus replied: 14

'It is true that I am testifying on my own behalf,
but my testimony is still valid,
because I know
where I came from and where I am going;
but you do not know
where I come from or where I am going.
You judge by human standards; 15
I judge no one,
but if I judge, 16
my judgement will be sound,
because I am not alone:

48

the one who sent me is with me;

17 and in your Law it is written
that the testimony of two witnesses is valid.

18 I may be testifying on my own behalf,
but the Father who sent me is my witness too.'

19 They asked him, 'Where is your Father?' Jesus
answered:

'You do not know me, nor do you know my
        Father;
if you did know me, you would know my
        Father as well'.

20 He spoke these words in the Treasury, while teaching
in the Temple. No one arrested him, because his time
had not yet come.

The unbelieving Jews warned

21 Again he said to them:

'I am going away; you will look for me
and you will die in your sin.
Where I am going, you cannot come.'

22 The Jews said to one another, 'Will he kill himself?
Is that what he means by saying, "Where I am going,
23 you cannot come"?' ·Jesus went on:

'You are from below;
I am from above.
You are of this world;
I am not of this world.

24 I have told you already: You will die in your
        sins.
Yes, if you do not believe that I am He,
you will die in your sins.'

So they said to him, 'Who are you?' Jesus answered: 25

'What I have told you from the outset.
About you I have much to say 26
and much to condemn;
but the one who sent me is truthful,
and what I have learnt from him
I declare to the world.'

They failed to understand that he was talking to them 27
about the Father. ·So Jesus said: 28

'When you have lifted up the Son of Man,
then you will know that I am He
and that I do nothing of myself:
what the Father has taught me
is what I preach;
he who sent me is with me, 29
and has not left me to myself,
for I always do what pleases him'.

As he was saying this, many came to believe in him. 30

Jesus and Abraham

To the Jews who believed in him Jesus said: 31

'If you make my word your home
you will indeed be my disciples,
you will learn the truth 32
and the truth will make you free'.

They answered, 'We are descended from Abraham 33
and we have never been the slaves of anyone; what do
you mean, "You will be made free"?' ·Jesus replied: 34

'I tell you most solemnly,
everyone who commits sin is a slave.

50

35 Now the slave's place in the house is not assured,
but the son's place is assured.

35 So if the Son makes you free,
you will be free indeed.

37 I know that you are descended from Abraham;
but in spite of that you want to kill me
because nothing I say has penetrated into you.

38 What I, for my part, speak of
is what I have seen with my Father;
but you, you put into action
the lessons learnt from your father.'

39 They repeated, 'Our father is Abraham'. Jesus said to them:

'If you were Abraham's children,
you would do as Abraham did.

40 As it is, you want to kill me
when I tell you the truth
as I have learnt it from God;
that is not what Abraham did.

41 What you are doing is what your father does.'

'We were not born of prostitution,'[a] they went on
42 'we have one father: God.' ·Jesus answered:

'If God were your father, you would love me,
since I have come here from God; yes, I have
come from him;
not that I came because I chose,
no, I was sent, and by him.

43 Do you know why you cannot take in what
I say?

8 a. By 'prostitution' the prophets often mean religious infidelity, cf.
Ho 1:2.

It is because you are unable to understand my
    language.
The devil is your father,   44
and you prefer to do
what your father wants.
He was a murderer from the start;
he was never grounded in the truth;
there is no truth in him at all:
when he lies
he is drawing on his own store,
because he is a liar, and the father of lies.
But as for me, I speak the truth   45
and for that very reason,
you do not believe me.   46
Can one of you convict me of sin?
If I speak the truth, why do you not believe me?
A child of God   47
listens to the words of God;
if you refuse to listen,
it is because you are not God's children.'

The Jews replied, 'Are we not right in saying that 48
you are a Samaritan and possessed by a devil?' Jesus
answered:

'I am not possessed;   49
no, I honour my Father,
but you want to dishonour me.
Not that I care for my own glory,   50
there is someone who takes care of that and is
    the judge of it.
I tell you most solemnly,   51
whoever keeps my word
will never see death.'

The Jews said, 'Now we know for certain that you are 52

possessed. Abraham is dead, and the prophets are dead,
and yet you say, "Whoever keeps my word will never
53 know the taste of death". ·Are you greater than our
father Abraham, who is dead? The prophets are dead
54 too. Who are you claiming to be?' ·Jesus answered:

'If I were to seek my own glory
that would be no glory at all;
my glory is conferred by the Father,
by the one of whom you say, "He is our God"
55 although you do not know him.
But I know him,
and if I were to say: I do not know him,
I should be a liar, as you are liars yourselves.
But I do know him, and I faithfully keep his
word.
56 Your father Abraham rejoiced
to think that he would see my Day;
he saw it and was glad.'

57 The Jews then said, 'You are not fifty yet, and you
58 have seen Abraham!' ·Jesus replied:

'I tell you most solemnly,
before Abraham ever was,
I Am'.

59 At this they picked up stones to throw at him;[b] but
Jesus hid himself and left the Temple.

The cure of the man born blind

1 **9** As he went along, he saw a man who had been blind
2 from birth. ·His disciples asked him, 'Rabbi, who
sinned, this man or his parents, for him to have been

b. Stoning was the penalty for blasphemy. Cf. 10:33.

born blind?' ·'Neither he nor his parents sinned,' Jesus 3
answered 'he was born blind so that the works of God
might be displayed in him.

'As long as the day lasts 4
I must carry out the work of the one who sent
    me;
the night will soon be here when no one can
    work.
As long as I am in the world 5
I am the light of the world.'

Having said this, he spat on the ground, made a paste 6
with the spittle, put this over the eyes of the blind man,
and said to him, 'Go and wash in the Pool of Siloam*a* 7
(a name that means 'sent'). So the blind man went off
and washed himself, and came away with his sight
restored.

His neighbours and people who earlier had seen him 8
begging said, 'Isn't this the man who used to sit and
beg?' ·Some said, 'Yes, it is the same one'. Others said, 9
'No, he only looks like him'. The man himself said, 'I
am the man'. ·So they said to him, 'Then how do your 10
eyes come to be open?' ·'The man called Jesus' he 11
answered 'made a paste, daubed my eyes with it and
said to me, "Go and wash at Siloam"; so I went, and
when I washed I could see.' ·They asked, 'Where is 12
he?' 'I don't know' he answered.

They brought the man who had been blind to the 13
Pharisees. ·It had been a sabbath day when Jesus made 14
the paste and opened the man's eyes, ·so when the 15
Pharisees asked him how he had come to see, he said,
'He put a paste on my eyes, and I washed, and I can
see'. ·Then some of the Pharisees said, 'This man 16
cannot be from God: he does not keep the sabbath'.

Others said, 'How could a sinner produce signs like
17 this?' And there was disagreement among them. ·So
they spoke to the blind man again, 'What have you to
say about him yourself, now that he has opened your
eyes?' 'He is a prophet' replied the man.

18   However, the Jews would not believe that the man
had been blind and had gained his sight, without first
19 sending for his parents and ·asking them, 'Is this man
really your son who you say was born blind? If so,
20 how is it that he is now able to see?' ·His parents
answered, 'We know he is our son and we know he was
21 born blind, ·but we don't know how it is that he can
see now, or who opened his eyes. He is old enough:
22 let him speak for himself.' ·His parents spoke like this
out of fear of the Jews, who had already agreed to
expel from the synagogue anyone who should acknow-
23 ledge Jesus as the Christ. ·This was why his parents
said, 'He is old enough; ask him'.

24   So the Jews again sent for the man and said to him,
'Give glory to God![b] For our part, we know that this
25 man is a sinner.' ·The man answered, 'I don't know if
he is a sinner; I only know that I was blind and now I
26 can see'. ·They said to him, 'What did he do to you?
27 How did he open your eyes?' ·He replied, 'I have told
you once and you wouldn't listen. Why do you want to
hear it all again? Do you want to become his disciples
28 too?' ·At this they hurled abuse at him: 'You can be
29 his disciple,' they said 'we are disciples of Moses: ·we
know that God spoke to Moses, but as for this man, we
30 don't know where he comes from'. ·The man replied,
'Now here is an astonishing thing! He has opened my

9 a. Water from this pool was drawn during the feast of Tabernacles
to symbolise the waters of blessing.
b. I.e. putting the man on oath.

eyes, and you don't know where he comes from! ·We 31
know that God doesn't listen to sinners, but God does
listen to men who are devout and do his will. ·Ever 32
since the world began it is unheard of for anyone to open
the eyes of a man who was born blind; ·if this man were 33
not from God, he couldn't do a thing.' ·'Are you trying 34
to teach us,' they replied 'and you a sinner through and
through, since you were born!' And they drove him
away.

Jesus heard they had driven him away, and when he 35
found him he said to him, 'Do you believe in the Son
of Man?' ·'Sir,' the man replied 'tell me who he is so 36
that I may believe in him.' ·Jesus said, 'You are looking 37
at him; he is speaking to you'. ·The man said, 'Lord, 38
I believe', and worshipped him.

Jesus said: 39

'It is for judgement
that I have come into this world,
so that those without sight may see
and those with sight turn blind'.

Hearing this, some Pharisees who were present said to 40
him, 'We are not blind, surely?' ·Jesus replied: 41

'Blind? If you were,
you would not be guilty,
but since you say, "We see",
your guilt remains.

The good shepherd

10 'I tell you most solemnly, anyone who does not 1
enter the sheepfold through the gate, but gets in
some other way is a thief and a brigand. ·The one who 2
enters through the gate is the shepherd of the flock;

3 the gatekeeper lets him in, the sheep hear his voice, one by one he calls his own sheep and leads them out.

4 When he has brought out his flock, he goes ahead of them, and the sheep follow because they know his voice.

5 They never follow a stranger but run away from him: they do not recognise the voice of strangers.'

6 Jesus told them[a] this parable but they failed to understand what he meant by telling it to them.

7 So Jesus spoke to them again:

'I tell you most solemnly,
I am the gate of the sheepfold.

8 All others who have come
are thieves and brigands;
but the sheep took no notice of them.

9 I am the gate.
Anyone who enters through me will be safe:
he will go freely in and out
and be sure of finding pasture.

10 The thief comes
only to steal and kill and destroy.
I have come
so that they may have life
and have it to the full.

11 I am the good shepherd:
the good shepherd is one who lays down his life
for his sheep.

12 The hired man, since he is not the shepherd
and the sheep do not belong to him,
abandons the sheep and runs away
as soon as he sees a wolf coming,
and then the wolf attacks and scatters the sheep;

13 this is because he is only a hired man

10 a. The Pharisees.

and has no concern for the sheep.
I am the good shepherd;   14
I know my own
and my own know me,
just as the Father knows me   15
and I know the Father;
and I lay down my life for my sheep.
And there are other sheep I have   16
that are not of this fold,
and these I have to lead as well.
They too will listen to my voice,
and there will be only one flock,
and one shepherd.
The Father loves me,   17
because I lay down my life
in order to take it up again.
No one takes it from me;   18
I lay it down of my own free will,
and as it is in my power to lay it down,
so it is in my power to take it up again;
and this is the command I have been given by
    my Father.'

These words caused disagreement among the Jews. 19
Many said, 'He is possessed, he is raving; why bother 20
to listen to him?' ·Others said, 'These are not the words 21
of a man possessed by a devil: could a devil open the
eyes of the blind?'

VI. THE FEAST OF DEDICATION

Jesus claims to be the Son of God

It was the time when the feast of Dedication was 22
being celebrated in Jerusalem. It was winter, ·and Jesus 23

was in the Temple walking up and down in the Portico
24 of Solomon. ·The Jews gathered round him and said,
'How much longer are you going to keep us in suspense?
25 If you are the Christ, tell us plainly.' ·Jesus replied:

'I have told you, but you do not believe.
The works I do in my Father's name are my
   witness;
26   but you do not believe,
   because you are no sheep of mine.
27   The sheep that belong to me listen to my voice;
   I know them and they follow me.
28   I give them eternal life;
   they will never be lost
   and no one will ever steal them from me.
29   The Father who gave them to me is greater than
         anyone,
   and no one can steal from the Father.
30   The Father and I are one.'

31
32 The Jews fetched stones to stone him, ·so Jesus said
to them, 'I have done many good works for you to see,
works from my Father; for which of these are you
33 stoning me?' ·The Jews answered him, 'We are not
stoning you for doing a good work but for blasphemy:
34 you are only a man and you claim to be God'. ·Jesus
answered:

'Is it not written in your Law:
I said, you are gods?[b]

35   So the Law uses the word gods
   of those to whom the word of God was
         addressed,
   and scripture cannot be rejected.
b. Ps 82:6.

Yet you say to someone the Father has 36
    consecrated and sent into the world,
"You are blaspheming",
because he says, "I am the Son of God".
If I am not doing my Father's work, 37
there is no need to believe me;
but if I am doing it, 38
then even if you refuse to believe in me,
at least believe in the work I do;
then you will know for sure
that the Father is in me and I am in the Father.'

They wanted to arrest him then, but he eluded them. 39

Jesus withdraws to the other side of the Jordan

He went back again to the far side of the Jordan to 40
stay in the district where John had once been baptising.
Many people who came to him there said, 'John gave 41
no signs, but all he said about this man was true'; ·and 42
many of them believed in him.

The resurrection of Lazarus

11 There was a man named Lazarus who lived in the 1
village of Bethany with the two sisters, Mary and
Martha, and he was ill.——·It was the same Mary, the 2
sister of the sick man Lazarus, who anointed the Lord
with ointment and wiped his feet with her hair. ·The 3
sisters sent this message to Jesus, 'Lord, the man you
love is ill'. ·On receiving the message, Jesus said, 'This 4
sickness will end not in death but in God's glory, and
through it the Son of God will be glorified'.

Jesus loved Martha and her sister and Lazarus, ·yet 5
when he heard that Lazarus was ill he stayed where he 6
was for two more days ·before saying to the disciples, 7

8 'Let us go to Judaea'. ·The disciples said, 'Rabbi, it is not long since the Jews wanted to stone you; are you
9 going back again?' ·Jesus replied:

'Are there not twelve hours in the day?
A man can walk in the daytime without
    stumbling
because he has the light of this world to see
    by;
10   but if he walks at night he stumbles,
because there is no light to guide him.'

11   He said that and then added, 'Our friend Lazarus is
12 resting, I am going to wake him'. ·The disciples said to him, 'Lord, if he is able to rest he is sure to get better'.
13 The phrase Jesus used referred to the death of Lazarus, but they thought that by 'rest' he meant 'sleep', so
14 Jesus put it plainly, 'Lazarus is dead; ·and for your
15 sake I am glad I was not there because now you will
16 believe. But let us go to him.' ·Then Thomas—known as the Twin—said to the other disciples, 'Let us go too, and die with him'.
17   On arriving, Jesus found that Lazarus had been in
18 the tomb for four days already. ·Bethany is only about
19 two miles from Jerusalem, ·and many Jews had come to Martha and Mary to sympathise with them over their
20 brother. ·When Martha heard that Jesus had come she went to meet him. Mary remained sitting in the house.
21 Martha said to Jesus, 'If you had been here, my
22 brother would not have died, ·but I know that, even now, whatever you ask of God, he will grant you'.
23 'Your brother' said Jesus to her 'will rise again.'
24 Martha said, 'I know he will rise again at the resur-
25 rection on the last day'. ·Jesus said:

'I am the resurrection.
If anyone believes in me, even though he dies
   he will live,
and whoever lives and believes in me   26
will never die.
Do you believe this?'

'Yes, Lord,' she said 'I believe that you are the Christ, 27
the Son of God, the one who was to come into this
world.'

When she had said this, she went and called her sister 28
Mary, saying in a low voice, 'The Master is here and
wants to see you'. ·Hearing this, Mary got up quickly 29
and went to him. ·Jesus had not yet come into the 30
village; he was still at the place where Martha had met
him. ·When the Jews who were in the house sympathis- 31
ing with Mary saw her get up so quickly and go out,
they followed her, thinking that she was going to the
tomb to weep there.

Mary went to Jesus, and as soon as she saw him she 32
threw herself at his feet, saying, 'Lord, if you had been
here, my brother would not have died'. ·At the sight of 33
her tears, and those of the Jews who followed her,
Jesus said in great distress, with a sigh that came
straight from the heart, ·'Where have you put him?' 34
They said, 'Lord, come and see'. ·Jesus wept; ·and the ³⁵₃₆
Jews said, 'See how much he loved him!' ·But there 37
were some who remarked, 'He opened the eyes of the
blind man, could he not have prevented this man's
death?' ·Still sighing, Jesus reached the tomb: it was a 38
cave with a stone to close the opening. ·Jesus said, 39
'Take the stone away'. Martha said to him, 'Lord, by
now he will smell; this is the fourth day'. ·Jesus replied, 40
'Have I not told you that if you believe you will see the

41 glory of God?' ·So they took away the stone. Then
Jesus lifted up his eyes and said:

> 'Father, I thank you for hearing my prayer.
42 I knew indeed that you always hear me,
> but I speak
> for the sake of all these who stand round me,
> so that they may believe it was you who sent me.'

43 When he had said this, he cried in a loud voice,
44 'Lazarus, here! Come out!' ·The dead man came out,
his feet and hands bound with bands of stuff and a
cloth round his face. Jesus said to them, 'Unbind him,
let him go free'.

The Jewish leaders decide on the death of Jesus

45 Many of the Jews who had come to visit Mary and
46 had seen what he did believed in him, ·but some of them
47 went to tell the Pharisees what Jesus had done. ·Then
the chief priests and Pharisees called a meeting. 'Here
is this man working all these signs' they said 'and what
48 action are we taking? ·If we let him go on in this way
everybody will believe in him, and the Romans will
49 come and destroy the Holy Place and our nation.' ·One
of them, Caiaphas, the high priest that year, said, 'You
50 don't seem to have grasped the situation at all; ·you fail
to see that it is better for one man to die for the people,
51 than for the whole nation to be destroyed'. ·He did not
speak in his own person, it was as high priest that he
made this prophecy that Jesus was to die for the nation
52 —·and not for the nation only, but to gather together
53 in unity the scattered children of God. ·From that day
54 they were determined to kill him. ·So Jesus no longer
went about openly among the Jews, but left the district

for a town called Ephraim, in the country bordering on
the desert, and stayed there with his disciples.

VII. THE LAST PASSOVER

A. BEFORE THE PASSION

The Passover draws near

The Jewish Passover drew near, and many of the 55
country people who had gone up to Jerusalem to purify
themselves ·looked out for Jesus, saying to one another 56
as they stood about in the Temple, 'What do you think?
Will he come to the festival or not?' ·The chief priests 57
and Pharisees had by now given their orders: anyone
who knew where he was must inform them so that they
could arrest him.

The anointing at Bethany

12 Six days before the Passover, Jesus went to 1
Bethany, where Lazarus was, whom he had raised
from the dead. ·They gave a dinner for him there; Martha 2
waited on them and Lazarus was among those at table.
Mary brought in a pound of very costly ointment, pure 3
nard, and with it anointed the feet of Jesus, wiping them
with her hair; the house was full of the scent of the ointment. ·Then Judas Iscariot—one of his disciples, the man 4
who was to betray him—said, ·'Why wasn't this ointment 5
sold for three hundred denarii, and the money given to
the poor?' ·He said this, not because he cared about the 6
poor, but because he was a thief; he was in charge of
the common fund and used to help himself to the
contributions. ·So Jesus said, 'Leave her alone; she had 7
to keep this scent for the day of my burial. ·You have 8
the poor with you always, you will not always have me.'

9 Meanwhile a large number of Jews heard that he was there and came not only on account of Jesus but also to see Lazarus whom he had raised from the dead.
10 Then the chief priests decided to kill Lazarus as well,
11 since it was on his account that many of the Jews were leaving them and believing in Jesus.

The Messiah enters Jerusalem

12 The next day the crowds who had come up for the festival heard that Jesus was on his way to Jerusalem.
13 They took branches of palm and went out to meet him, shouting, '*Hosanna! Blessings on* the King of
14 Israel, *who comes in the name of the Lord.*'[a] ·Jesus found a young donkey and mounted it—as scripture says:
15 *Do not be afraid, daughter of Zion; see, your king is*
16 *coming, mounted on the colt of a donkey.*[b] ·At the time his disciples did not understand this, but later, after Jesus had been glorified, they remembered that this had been written about him and that this was in fact how
17 they had received him. ·All who had been with him when he called Lazarus out of the tomb and raised him from the dead were telling how they had witnessed it;
18 it was because of this, too, that the crowd came out to meet him: they had heard that he had given this sign.
19 Then the Pharisees said to one another, 'You see, there is nothing you can do; look, the whole world is running after him!'

Jesus foretells his death and subsequent glorification

20 Among those who went up to worship at the festival
21 were some Greeks.[c] ·These approached Philip, who came from Bethsaida in Galilee, and put this request to

12 a. Ps 118:26.   **b.** Zc 9:9f.   **c.** The 'God-fearing men' of Ac 10:2: converts who observed certain specific Mosaic observances.

him, 'Sir, we should like to see Jesus'. ·Philip went to 22
tell Andrew, and Andrew and Philip together went to
tell Jesus.

Jesus replied to them: 23

'Now the hour has come
for the Son of Man to be glorified.
I tell you, most solemnly, 24
unless a wheat grain falls on the ground and
dies,
it remains only a single grain;
but if it dies,
it yields a rich harvest.
Anyone who loves his life loses it; 25
anyone who hates his life in this world
will keep it for the eternal life.
If a man serves me, he must follow me, 26
wherever I am, my servant will be there too.
If anyone serves me, my Father will honour him.
Now my soul is troubled. 27
What shall I say:
Father, save me from this hour?
But it was for this very reason that I have come
to this hour.
Father, glorify your name!' 28

A voice came from heaven, 'I have glorified it, and I
will glorify it again'.

People standing by, who heard this, said it was a clap 29
of thunder; others said, 'It was an angel speaking to
him'. ·Jesus answered, 'It was not for my sake that this 30
voice came, but for yours.

'Now sentence is being passed on this world; 31
now the prince of this world is to be
overthrown.*

32   And when I am lifted up from the earth,
       I shall draw all men to myself.'

33   By these words he indicated the kind of death he
34 would die. ·The crowd answered, 'The Law has taught
   us that the Christ will remain for ever. How can you
   say, "The Son of Man must be lifted up"? Who is this
35 Son of Man?' ·Jesus then said:

       'The light will be with you only a little longer
           now.
       Walk while you have the light,
       or the dark will overtake you;
       he who walks in the dark does not know where
           he is going.
36   While you still have the light,
       believe in the light
       and you will become sons of light.'

   Having said this, Jesus left them and kept himself
   hidden.

Conclusion: the unbelief of the Jews

37   Though they had been present when he gave so many
38 signs, they did not believe in him; ·this was to fulfil the
   words of the prophet Isaiah: *Lord, who could believe
   what we have heard said, and to whom has the power of
39 the Lord been revealed?*[e] ·Indeed, they were unable to
40 believe because, as Isaiah says again: ·*He has blinded
   their eyes, he has hardened their heart, for fear they
   should see with their eyes and understand with their heart,
   and turn to me for healing.*[f]
41   Isaiah said this when he saw his glory,[g] and his words
   referred to Jesus.

d. Satan.   **e.** Is 53:1.   **f.** Is 6:9f.   **g.** Isaiah's vision in the
Temple, Is 6:4, interpreted as a prophetic vision of Christ's glory.

And yet there were many who did believe in him, 42
even among the leading men, but they did not admit it,
through fear of the Pharisees and fear of being expelled
from the synagogue: ·they put honour from men before 43
the honour that comes from God.

Jesus declared publicly: 44

'Whoever believes in me
believes not in me
but in the one who sent me,
and whoever sees me, 45
sees the one who sent me.
I, the light, have come into the world, 46
so that whoever believes in me
need not stay in the dark any more.
If anyone hears my words and does not keep 47
them faithfully,
it is not I who shall condemn him,
since I have come not to condemn the world,
but to save the world:
he who rejects me and refuses my words 48
has his judge already:
the word itself that I have spoken
will be his judge on the last day.
For what I have spoken does not come from 49
myself;
no, what I was to say, what I had to speak,
was commanded by the Father who sent me,
and I know that his commands mean eternal life. 50
And therefore what the Father has told me
is what I speak.'

B. THE LAST SUPPER

Jesus washes his disciples' feet

1 13 It was before the festival of the Passover, and Jesus knew that the hour had come for him to pass from this world to the Father. He had always loved those who were his in the world, but now he showed how perfect his love was.

2 They were at supper, and the devil had already put it into the mind of Judas Iscariot son of Simon, to

3 betray him. ·Jesus knew that the Father had put everything into his hands, and that he had come from God

4 and was returning to God, ·and he got up from table, removed his outer garment and, taking a towel, wrapped

5 it round his waist; ·he then poured water into a basin and began to wash the disciples' feet[a] and to wipe them with the towel he was wearing.

6 He came to Simon Peter, who said to him, 'Lord, are

7 you going to wash my feet?' ·Jesus answered, 'At the moment you do not know what I am doing, but later

8 you will understand'. ·'Never!' said Peter. 'You shall never wash my feet.' Jesus replied, 'If I do not wash

9 you, you can have nothing in common with me'. ·'Then, Lord,' said Simon Peter 'not only my feet, but my hands

10 and my head as well!' ·Jesus said, 'No one who has taken a bath needs washing, he is clean all over. You

11 too are clean, though not all of you are.' ·He knew who was going to betray him, that was why he said, 'though not all of you are'.

12 When he had washed their feet and put on his clothes again he went back to the table. 'Do you understand'

13 he said 'what I have done to you? ·You call me Master

13 a. The dress and the duty are those of a slave.

and Lord, and rightly; so I am. ·If I, then, the Lord and 14
Master, have washed your feet, you should wash each
other's feet. ·I have given you an example so that you 15
may copy what I have done to you.

> 'I tell you most solemnly, 16
> no servant is greater than his master,
> no messenger is greater than the man who sent
>   him.

'Now that you know this, happiness will be yours if 17
you behave accordingly. ·I am not speaking about all of 18
you: I know the ones I have chosen; but what scripture
says must be fulfilled: *Someone who shares my table
rebels against me.*[b]

> 'I tell you this now, before it happens, 19
> so that when it does happen
> you may believe that I am He.
> I tell you most solemnly, 20
> whoever welcomes the one I send welcomes me,
> and whoever welcomes me welcomes the one
>   who sent me.'

The treachery of Judas foretold

Having said this, Jesus was troubled in spirit and 21
declared, 'I tell you most solemnly, one of you will
betray me'. ·The disciples looked at one another, 22
wondering which he meant. ·The disciple Jesus loved 23
was reclining next to Jesus; ·Simon Peter signed to him 24
and said, 'Ask who it is he means', ·so leaning back on 25
Jesus' breast he said, 'Who is it, Lord?' ·'It is the one' 26
replied Jesus 'to whom I give the piece of bread that I
shall dip in the dish.' He dipped the piece of bread and
gave it to Judas son of Simon Iscariot. ·At that instant, 27
after Judas had taken the bread, Satan entered him.

Jesus then said, 'What you are going to do, do quickly'.
28 None of the others at table understood the reason he
29 said this. ·Since Judas had charge of the common fund,
some of them thought Jesus was telling him, 'Buy what
we need for the festival', or telling him to give some-
30 thing to the poor. ·As soon as Judas had taken the piece
of bread he went out. Night had fallen.
31 When he had gone Jesus said:

'Now has the Son of Man been glorified,
and in him God has been glorified.
32 If God has been glorified in him,
God will in turn glorify him in himself,[c]
and will glorify him very soon.

Farewell discourses

33 'My little children,
I shall not be with you much longer.
You will look for me,
and, as I told the Jews,
where I am going,
you cannot come.
34 I give you a new commandment:
love one another;
just as I have loved you,
you also must love one another.
35 By this love you have for one another,
everyone will know that you are my disciples.'

36 Simon Peter said, 'Lord, where are you going?' Jesus
replied, 'Where I am going you cannot follow me now;
37 you will follow me later'. ·Peter said to him, 'Why can't
I follow you now? I will lay down my life for you.'

b. Ps 41:9.
c. I.e. the Father will take the Son of Man to himself in glory.

'Lay down your life for me?' answered Jesus. 'I tell you 38
most solemnly, before the cock crows you will have
disowned me three times.

14 'Do not let your hearts be troubled.   1
Trust in God still, and trust in me.
There are many rooms in my Father's house;   2
if there were not, I should have told you.
I am going now to prepare a place for you,
and after I have gone and prepared you a place,   3
I shall return to take you with me;
so that where I am
you may be too.
You know the way to the place where I am   4
going.'

Thomas said, 'Lord, we do not know where you are   5
going, so how can we know the way?' ·Jesus said: 6

'I am the Way, the Truth and the Life.
No one can come to the Father except through
me.
If you know me, you know my Father too.   7
From this moment you know him and have
seen him.'

Philip said, 'Lord, let us see the Father and then we 8
shall be satisfied'. ·'Have I been with you all this time, 9
Philip,' said Jesus to him 'and you still do not know me?

'To have seen me is to have seen the Father,
so how can you say, "Let us see the Father"?
Do you not believe   10
that I am in the Father and the Father is in me?
The words I say to you I do not speak as from
myself:

it is the Father, living in me, who is doing this
    work.

11   You must believe me when I say
that I am in the Father and the Father is in me;
believe it on the evidence of this work, if for
    no other reason.

12   I tell you most solemnly,
whoever believes in me
will perform the same works as I do myself,
he will perform even greater works,
because I am going to the Father.

13   Whatever you ask for in my name I will do,
so that the Father may be glorified in the Son.

14   If you ask for anything in my name,
I will do it.

15   If you love me you will keep my commandments.

16   I shall ask the Father,
and he will give you another Advocate[a]
to be with you for ever,

17   that Spirit of truth
whom the world can never receive
since it neither sees nor knows him;
but you know him,
because he is with you, he is in you.

18   I will not leave you orphans;
I will come back to you.

19   In a short time the world will no longer see me;
but you will see me,
because I live and you will live.

20   On that day
you will understand that I am in my Father
and you in me and I in you.

14 a. Greek *parakletos*: advocate or counsellor or protector.

Anybody who receives my commandments and   21
    keeps them
will be one who loves me;
and anybody who loves me will be loved by my
    Father,
and I shall love him and show myself to him.'

Judas[b]—this was not Judas Iscariot—said to him, 22
'Lord, what is all this about? Do you intend to show
yourself to us and not to the world?' ·Jesus replied: 23

'If anyone loves me he will keep my word,
and my Father will love him,
and we shall come to him
and make our home with him.
Those who do not love me do not keep my   24
    words.
And my word is not my own:
it is the word of the one who sent me.
I have said these things to you   25
while still with you;
but the Advocate, the Holy Spirit,   26
whom the Father will send in my name,
will teach you everything
and remind you of all I have said to you.
Peace[c] I bequeath to you,   27
my own peace I give you,
a peace the world cannot give, this is my gift
    to you.
Do not let your hearts be troubled or afraid.
You heard me say: 28
I am going away, and shall return.
If you loved me you would have been glad to
    know that I am going to the Father,

for the Father is greater than I.

29 I have told you this now before it happens,
so that when it does happen you may believe.

30 I shall not talk with you any longer,
because the prince of this world is on his way.
He has no power over me,

31 but the world must be brought to know that I
love the Father
and that I am doing exactly what the Father
told me.
Come now, let us go.

The true vine

1 **15** 'I am the true vine,
and my Father is the vinedresser.

2 Every branch in me that bears no fruit
he cuts away,
and every branch that does bear fruit he prunes
to make it bear even more.

3 You are pruned already,
by means of the word that I have spoken to you.

4 Make your home in me, as I make mine in you.
As a branch cannot bear fruit all by itself,
but must remain part of the vine,
neither can you unless you remain in me.

5 I am the vine,
you are the branches.
Whoever remains in me, with me in him,
bears fruit in plenty;
for cut off from me you can do nothing.

6 Anyone who does not remain in me

b. 'Judas, brother of James' in Lk 6:16 and Ac 1:13; the Thaddaeus
of Mt 10:3 and Mk 3:18.   **c.** The customary Jewish farewell.

is like a branch that has been thrown away
—he withers;
these branches are collected and thrown on the
    fire,
and they are burnt.
If you remain in me   7
and my words remain in you,
you may ask what you will
and you shall get it.
It is to the glory of my Father that you should   8
    bear much fruit,
and then you will be my disciples.
As the Father has loved me,   9
so I have loved you.
Remain in my love.
If you keep my commandments   10
you will remain in my love,
just as I have kept my Father's commandments
and remain in his love.
I have told you this   11
so that my own joy may be in you
and your joy be complete.
This is my commandment: 12
love one another,
as I have loved you.
A man can have no greater love   13
than to lay down his life for his friends.
You are my friends,   14
if you do what I command you.
I shall not call you servants any more,   15
because a servant does not know
his master's business;
I call you friends,
because I have made known to you

everything I have learnt from my Father.

16 You did not choose me,
no, I chose you;
and I commissioned you
to go out and to bear fruit,
fruit that will last;
and then the Father will give you
anything you ask him in my name.

17 What I command you
is to love one another.

The hostile world

18 'If the world hates you,
remember that it hated me before you.

19 If you belonged to the world,
the world would love you as its own;
but because you do not belong to the world,
because my choice withdrew you from the world,
therefore the world hates you.

20 Remember the words I said to you:
A servant is not greater than his master.
If they persecuted me,
they will persecute you too;
if they kept my word,
they will keep yours as well.

21 But it will be on my account that they will do
     all this,
because they do not know the one who sent me.

22 If I had not come,
if I had not spoken to them,
they would have been blameless;
but as it is they have no excuse for their sin.

23 Anyone who hates me hates my Father.

24 If I had not performed such works among them

as no one else has ever done,
they would be blameless;
but as it is, they have seen all this,
and still they hate both me and my Father.
But all this was only to fulfil the words written 25
in their Law:
They hated me for no reason.^a
When the Advocate comes, 26
whom I shall send to you from the Father,
the Spirit of truth who issues from the Father,
he will be my witness.
And you too will be witnesses, 27
because you have been with me from the outset.

16

'I have told you all this 1
so that your faith may not be shaken.
They will expel you from the synagogues, 2
and indeed the hour is coming
when anyone who kills you will think he is doing
a holy duty for God.
They will do these things 3
because they have never known either the Father
or myself.
But I have told you all this, 4
so that when the time for it comes
you may remember that I told you.

The coming of the Advocate

'I did not tell you this from the outset,
because I was with you;
but now I am going to the one who sent me. 5
Not one of you has asked, "Where are you
going?"

6   Yet you are sad at heart because I have told
        you this.

7   Still, I must tell you the truth:
    it is for your own good that I am going
    because unless I go,
    the Advocate will not come to you;
    but if I do go,
    I will send him to you.

8   And when he comes,
    he will show the world how wrong it was,
    about sin,
    and about who was in the right,
    and about judgement:

9   about sin:
    proved by their refusal to believe in me;

10   about who was in the right:
    proved by my going to the Father
    and your seeing me no more;

11   about judgement:
    proved by the prince of this world being already
        condemned.

12   I still have many things to say to you
    but they would be too much for you now.

13   But when the Spirit of truth comes
    he will lead you to the complete truth,
    since he will not be speaking as from himself
    but will say only what he has learnt;
    and he will tell you of the things to come.

14   He will glorify me,
    since all he tells you
    will be taken from what is mine.

15   Everything the Father has is mine;
    that is why I said:

15 a. Ps 35:19.

All he tells you
will be taken from what is mine.

Jesus to return very soon

'In a short time you will no longer see me,   16
and then a short time later you will see me
        again.'

Then some of his disciples said to one another, 'What 17
does he mean, "In a short time you will no longer see me,
and then a short time later you will see me again" and, "I
am going to the Father"? ·What is this "short time"? 18
We don't know what he means.' ·Jesus knew that they 19
wanted to question him, so he said, 'You are asking one
another what I meant by saying: In a short time you
will no longer see me, and then a short time later you
will see me again.

'I tell you most solemnly,   20
you will be weeping and wailing
while the world will rejoice;
you will be sorrowful,
but your sorrow will turn to joy.
A woman in childbirth suffers,   21
because her time has come;
but when she has given birth to the child she
        forgets the suffering
in her joy that a man has been born into the
        world.
So it is with you: you are sad now,   22
but I shall see you again, and your hearts will
        be full of joy,
and that joy no one shall take from you.
When that day comes,   23
you will not ask me any questions.

I tell you most solemnly,
anything you ask for from the Father
he will grant in my name.
24 Until now you have not asked for anything in
my name.
Ask and you will receive,
and so your joy will be complete.
25 I have been telling you all this in metaphors,
the hour is coming
when I shall no longer speak to you in
metaphors;
but tell you about the Father in plain words.
26 When that day comes
you will ask in my name;
and I do not say that I shall pray to the Father
for you,
27 because the Father himself loves you
for loving me
and believing that I came from God.
28 I came from the Father and have come into
the world
and now I leave the world to go to the Father.'

29 His disciples said, 'Now you are speaking plainly and
30 not using metaphors! ·Now we see that you know
everything, and do not have to wait for questions to be
put into words; because of this we believe that you
31 came from God.' ·Jesus answered them:

'Do you believe at last?
32 Listen; the time will come—in fact it has come
already—
when you will be scattered, each going his own
way
and leaving me alone.

And yet I am not alone,
because the Father is with me.
I have told you all this   33
so that you may find peace in me.
In the world you will have trouble,
but be brave:
I have conquered the world.'

The priestly prayer of Christ

17 After saying this, Jesus raised his eyes to heaven
and said:

'Father, the hour has come: 1
glorify your Son
so that your Son may glorify you;
and, through the power over all mankind*a* that   2
    you have given him,
let him give eternal life to all those you have
    entrusted to him.
And eternal life is this: 3
to know you,
the only true God,
and Jesus Christ whom you have sent.
I have glorified you on earth   4
and finished the work
that you gave me to do.
Now, Father, it is time for you to glorify me   5
with that glory I had with you
before ever the world was.
I have made your name known   6
to the men you took from the world to give me.
They were yours and you gave them to me,
and they have kept your word.
Now at last they know   7

that all you have given me comes indeed from
    you;
8   for I have given them
the teaching you gave to me,
and they have truly accepted this, that I came
    from you,
and have believed that it was you who sent me.
9   I pray for them;
I am not praying for the world
but for those you have given me,
because they belong to you:
10   all I have is yours
and all you have is mine,
and in them I am glorified.
11   I am not in the world any longer,
but they are in the world,
and I am coming to you.
Holy Father,
keep those you have given me true to your name,
so that they may be one like us.
12   While I was with them,
I kept those you had given me true to your
    name.
I have watched over them and not one is lost
except the one who chose to be lost,[b]
and this was to fulfil the scriptures.
13   But now I am coming to you
and while still in the world I say these things
to share my joy with them to the full.
14   I passed your word on to them,
and the world hated them,
because they belong to the world
no more than I belong to the world.

17 a. Lit. 'all flesh'.   b. Lit. 'the son of perdition'.

I am not asking you to remove them from the 15
world,
but to protect them from the evil one.
They do not belong to the world 16
any more than I belong to the world.
Consecrate them in the truth; 17
your word is truth.
As you sent me into the world, 18
I have sent them into the world,
and for their sake I consecrate myself 19
so that they too may be consecrated in truth.
I pray not only for these, 20
but for those also
who through their words will believe in me.
May they all be one. 21
Father, may they be one in us,
as you are in me and I am in you,
so that the world may believe it was you who
sent me.
I have given them the glory you gave to me, 22
that they may be one as we are one.
With me in them and you in me, 23
may they be so completely one
that the world will realise that it was you who
sent me
and that I have loved them as much as you
loved me.
Father, 24
I want those you have given me
to be with me where I am,
so that they may always see the glory
you have given me
because you loved me
before the foundation of the world.

25   Father, Righteous One,
        the world has not known you,
        but I have known you,
        and these have known
        that you have sent me.

26   I have made your name known to them
        and will continue to make it known,
        so that the love with which you loved me may
            be in them,
        and so that I may be in them.'

C. THE PASSION

The arrest of Jesus

1 **18** After he had said all this Jesus left with his disciples and crossed the Kedron valley. There was a garden 2 there, and he went into it with his disciples. ·Judas the traitor knew the place well, since Jesus had often met 3 his disciples there, ·and he brought the cohort[a] to this place together with a detachment of guards sent by the chief priests and the Pharisees, all with lanterns and 4 torches and weapons. ·Knowing everything that was going to happen to him, Jesus then came forward and 5 said, 'Who are you looking for?' ·They answered, 'Jesus the Nazarene'. He said, 'I am he'. Now Judas 6 the traitor was standing among them. ·When Jesus said, 7 'I am he', they moved back and fell to the ground. ·He asked them a second time, 'Who are you looking for?' 8 They said, 'Jesus the Nazarene'. ·'I have told you that I am he' replied Jesus. 'If I am the one you are looking 9 for, let these others go.' ·This was to fulfil the words he had spoken, 'Not one of those you gave me have I lost'.

18 a. A detachment from the Roman garrison in Jerusalem.

Simon Peter, who carried a sword, drew it and 10
wounded the high priest's servant, cutting off his right
ear. The servant's name was Malchus. ·Jesus said to 11
Peter, 'Put your sword back in its scabbard; am I not
to drink the cup that the Father has given me?'

Jesus before Annas and Caiaphas. Peter disowns him

The cohort and its captain and the Jewish guards 12
seized Jesus and bound him. ·They took him first to 13
Annas, because Annas was the father-in-law of Caiaphas, who was high priest that year. ·It was Caiaphas 14
who had suggested to the Jews, 'It is better for one man
to die for the people'.

Simon Peter, with another disciple, followed Jesus. 15
This disciple, who was known to the high priest, went
with Jesus into the high priest's palace, ·but Peter 16
stayed outside the door. So the other disciple, the one
known to the high priest, went out, spoke to the woman
who was keeping the door and brought Peter in. ·The 17
maid on duty at the door said to Peter, 'Aren't you
another of that man's disciples?' He answered, 'I am
not'. ·Now it was cold, and the servants and guards 18
had lit a charcoal fire and were standing there warming
themselves; so Peter stood there too, warming himself
with the others.

The high priest questioned Jesus about his disciples 19
and his teaching. ·Jesus answered, 'I have spoken openly 20
for all the world to hear; I have always taught in the
synagogue and in the Temple where all the Jews meet
together: I have said nothing in secret. ·But why ask 21
me? Ask my hearers what I taught: they know what I
said.' ·At these words, one of the guards standing by 22
gave Jesus a slap in the face, saying, 'Is that the way to
answer the high priest?' ·Jesus replied, 'If there is 23

something wrong in what I said, point it out; but if
24 there is no offence in it, why do you strike me?' ·Then
Annas sent him, still bound, to Caiaphas the high priest.

25   As Simon Peter stood there warming himself, someone said to him, 'Aren't you another of his disciples?'
26 He denied it saying, 'I am not'. ·One of the high
priest's servants, a relation of the man whose ear Peter
had cut off, said, 'Didn't I see you in the garden with
27 him?' ·Again Peter denied it; and at once a cock crew.

Jesus before Pilate

28   They then led Jesus from the house of Caiaphas to the
Praetorium.*b* It was now morning. They did not go into
the Praetorium themselves or they would be defiled*c*
29 and unable to eat the passover. ·So Pilate came outside
to them and said, 'What charge do you bring against
30 this man?' They replied, ·'If he were not a criminal, we
31 should not be handing him over to you'. ·Pilate said,
'Take him yourselves, and try him by your own Law'.
The Jews answered, 'We are not allowed to put a man
32 to death'. ·This was to fulfil the words Jesus had spoken
indicating the way he was going to die.

33   So Pilate went back into the Praetorium and called
Jesus to him, 'Are you the king of the Jews?' he asked.
34 Jesus replied, 'Do you ask this of your own accord, or
35 have others spoken to you about me?' ·Pilate answered,
'Am I a Jew? It is your own people and the chief priests
who have handed you over to me: what have you
36 done?' ·Jesus replied, 'Mine is not a kingdom of this
world; if my kingdom were of this world, my men
would have fought to prevent my being surrendered to
37 the Jews. But my kingdom is not of this kind.' ·'So you

b. The judicial court of the Roman procurator.   c. By entering the
house of a pagan. Cf. Lk 7:6.

are a king then?' said Pilate. 'It is you who say it'
answered Jesus. 'Yes, I am a king. I was born for this,
I came into the world for this: to bear witness to the
truth; and all who are on the side of truth listen to my
voice.' ·'Truth?' said Pilate. 'What is that?'; and with 38
that he went out again to the Jews and said, 'I find no
case against him. ·But according to a custom of yours 39
I should release one prisoner at the Passover; would
you like me, then, to release the king of the Jews?' ·At 40
this they shouted: 'Not this man,' they said 'but
Barabbas'. Barabbas was a brigand.

19 Pilate then had Jesus taken away and scourged; 1
and after this, the soldiers twisted some thorns into 2
a crown and put it on his head, and dressed him in a
purple robe. ·They kept coming up to him and saying, 3
'Hail, king of the Jews!'; and they slapped him in the
face.

Pilate came outside again and said to them, 'Look, 4
I am going to bring him out to you to let you see that
I find no case'. ·Jesus then came out wearing the crown 5
of thorns and the purple robe. Pilate said, 'Here is the
man'. ·When they saw him the chief priests and the 6
guards shouted, 'Crucify him! Crucify him!' Pilate
said, 'Take him yourselves and crucify him: I can find
no case against him'. ·'We have a Law,' the Jews replied 7
'and according to that Law he ought to die, because
he has claimed to be the Son of God.'

When Pilate heard them say this his fears increased. 8
Re-entering the Praetorium, he said to Jesus, 'Where 9
do you come from?' But Jesus made no answer.
Pilate then said to him, 'Are you refusing to speak to 10
me? Surely you know I have power to release you and
I have power to crucify you?' ·'You would have no 11

power over me' replied Jesus 'if it had not been given you from above; that is why the one who handed me over to you has the greater guilt.'

Jesus is condemned to death

12 From that moment Pilate was anxious to set him free, but the Jews shouted, 'If you set him free you are no friend of Caesar's; anyone who makes himself king is
13 defying Caesar'. ·Hearing these words, Pilate had Jesus brought out, and seated himself on the chair of judgement at a place called the Pavement, in Hebrew Gab-
14 batha. ·It was Passover Preparation Day, about the sixth hour.*ᵃ 'Here is your king' said Pilate to the Jews.
15 'Take him away, take him away!' they said. 'Crucify him!' 'Do you want me to crucify your king?' said Pilate. The chief priests answered, 'We have no king
16 except Caesar'. ·So in the end Pilate handed him over to them to be crucified.

The crucifixion

17 They then took charge of Jesus, ·and carrying his own cross he went out of the city to the place of the skull or,
18 as it was called in Hebrew, Golgotha, ·where they crucified him with two others, one on either side with
19 Jesus in the middle. ·Pilate wrote out a notice and had it fixed to the cross; it ran: 'Jesus the Nazarene, King
20 of the Jews'. ·This notice was read by many of the Jews, because the place where Jesus was crucified was not far from the city, and the writing was in Hebrew, Latin and
21 Greek. ·So the Jewish chief priests said to Pilate, 'You

19 a. On Preparation Day, the Passover supper was made ready for eating after sunset. The sixth hour is midday, by which time all leaven had to be removed from the house; during the feast only unleavened bread was eaten.

should not write "King of the Jews", but "This man said: I am King of the Jews" '. ·Pilate answered, 'What 22 I have written, I have written'.

Christ's garments divided

When the soldiers had finished crucifying Jesus they 23 took his clothing and divided it into four shares, one for each soldier. His undergarment was seamless, woven in one piece from neck to hem; ·so they said to one 24 another, 'Instead of tearing it, let's throw dice to decide who is to have it'. In this way the words of scripture were fulfilled:

They shared out my clothing among them.
They cast lots for my clothes.[b]

This is exactly what the soldiers did.

Jesus and his mother

Near the cross of Jesus stood his mother and his 25 mother's sister, Mary the wife of Clopas, and Mary of Magdala. ·Seeing his mother and the disciple he loved 26 standing near her, Jesus said to his mother, 'Woman, this is your son'. ·Then to the disciple he said, 'This is 27 your mother'. And from that moment the disciple made a place for her in his home.

The death of Jesus

After this, Jesus knew that everything had now been 28 completed, and to fulfil the scripture perfectly he said:

'I am thirsty'.[c]

A jar full of vinegar stood there, so putting a sponge 29 soaked in the vinegar on a hyssop stick they held it up to his mouth. ·After Jesus had taken the vinegar he 30 said, 'It is accomplished'; and bowing his head he gave up his spirit.

The pierced Christ

31 It was Preparation Day, and to prevent the bodies remaining on the cross during the sabbath—since that sabbath was a day of special solemnity—the Jews asked Pilate to have the legs broken*a* and the bodies taken
32 away. ·Consequently the soldiers came and broke the legs of the first man who had been crucified with him
33 and then of the other. ·When they came to Jesus, they found he was already dead, and so instead of breaking
34 his legs ·one of the soldiers pierced his side with a lance;
35 and immediately there came out blood and water. ·This is the evidence of one who saw it—trustworthy evidence, and he knows he speaks the truth—and he gives it so
36 that you may believe as well. ·Because all this happened to fulfil the words of scripture:

*Not one bone of his will be broken;*e

37 and again, in another place scripture says:

*They will look on the one whom they have pierced.*f

The burial

38 After this, Joseph of Arimathaea, who was a disciple of Jesus—though a secret one because he was afraid of the Jews—asked Pilate to let him remove the body of Jesus. Pilate gave permission, so they came and took it
39 away. ·Nicodemus came as well—the same one who had first come to Jesus at night-time—and he brought a

b. Ps 22:18.   **c.** Ps 22:15.   **d.** To hasten death.   **e.** Two texts are here combined: Ps 34:20 and Ex 12:46. The allusion is both to God protecting the good man, and to the ritual for preparing the Passover lamb.   **f.** Zc 12:10.

mixture of myrrh and aloes, weighing about a hundred pounds. ·They took the body of Jesus and wrapped it 40 with the spices in linen cloths, following the Jewish burial custom. ·At the place where he had been crucified 41 there was a garden, and in this garden a new tomb in which no one had yet been buried. ·Since it was the 42 Jewish Day of Preparation and the tomb was near at hand, they laid Jesus there.

VIII. THE DAY OF CHRIST'S RESURRECTION

The empty tomb

20 It was very early on the first day of the week and 1 still dark, when Mary of Magdala came to the tomb. She saw that the stone had been moved away from the tomb ·and came running to Simon Peter and 2 the other disciple, the one Jesus loved. 'They have taken the Lord out of the tomb' she said 'and we don't know where they have put him.'

So Peter set out with the other disciple to go to the 3 tomb. ·They ran together, but the other disciple, 4 running faster than Peter, reached the tomb first; ·he 5 bent down and saw the linen cloths lying on the ground, but did not go in. ·Simon Peter who was following now 6 came up, went right into the tomb, saw the linen cloths on the ground, ·and also the cloth that had been over 7 his head; this was not with the linen cloths but rolled up in a place by itself. ·Then the other disciple who had 8 reached the tomb first also went in; he saw and he believed. ·Till this moment they had failed to understand 9 the teaching of scripture, that he must rise from the dead. ·The disciples then went home again. 10

The appearance to Mary of Magdala

11 Meanwhile Mary stayed outside near the tomb, weeping. Then, still weeping, she stooped to look inside,
12 and saw two angels in white sitting where the body of Jesus had been, one at the head, the other at the feet.
13 They said, 'Woman, why are you weeping?' 'They have taken my Lord away' she replied 'and I don't
14 know where they have put him.' ·As she said this she turned round and saw Jesus standing there, though she
15 did not recognise him. ·Jesus said, 'Woman, why are you weeping? Who are you looking for?' Supposing him to be the gardener, she said, 'Sir, if you have taken him away, tell me where you have put him, and I will
16 go and remove him'. ·Jesus said, 'Mary!' She knew him then and said to him in Hebrew, 'Rabbuni!'—which
17 means Master. ·Jesus said to her, 'Do not cling to me, because I have not yet ascended to the Father. But go and find the brothers, and tell them: I am ascending to my Father and your Father, to my God and your God.'
18 So Mary of Magdala went and told the disciples that she had seen the Lord and that he had said these things to her.

Appearances to the disciples

19 In the evening of that same day, the first day of the week, the doors were closed in the room where the disciples were, for fear of the Jews. Jesus came and stood among them. He said to them, 'Peace be with
20 you', ·and showed them his hands and his side. The disciples were filled with joy when they saw the Lord,
21 and he said to them again, 'Peace be with you.

'As the Father sent me,
so am I sending you.'

After saying this he breathed on them and said: 22

> 'Receive the Holy Spirit.
> For those whose sins you forgive, 23
> they are forgiven;
> for those whose sins you retain,
> they are retained.'

Thomas, called the Twin, who was one of the Twelve, 24
was not with them when Jesus came. ·When the 25
disciples said, 'We have seen the Lord', he answered,
'Unless I see the holes that the nails made in his hands
and can put my finger into the holes they made, and
unless I can put my hand into his side, I refuse to
believe'. ·Eight days later the disciples were in the house 26
again and Thomas was with them. The doors were
closed, but Jesus came in and stood among them.
'Peace be with you' he said. ·Then he spoke to Thomas, 27
'Put your finger here; look, here are my hands. Give me
your hand; put it into my side. Doubt no longer but
believe.' ·Thomas replied, 'My Lord and my God!' 28
Jesus said to him: 29

> 'You believe because you can see me.
> Happy are those who have not seen and yet
> believe.'

CONCLUSION

There were many other signs that Jesus worked and 30
the disciples saw, but they are not recorded in this book.
These are recorded so that you may believe that Jesus 31
is the Christ, the Son of God, and that believing this
you may have life through his name.

APPENDIX[a]

The appearance on the shore of Tiberias

1 21 Later on, Jesus showed himself again to the disciples. It was by the Sea of Tiberias, and it hap-
2 pened like this: ·Simon Peter, Thomas called the Twin,
Nathanael from Cana in Galilee, the sons of Zebedee
3 and two more of his disciples were together. ·Simon
Peter said, 'I'm going fishing'. They replied, 'We'll come
with you'. They went out and got into the boat but
caught nothing that night.

4 It was light by now and there stood Jesus on the
shore, though the disciples did not realise that it was
5 Jesus. ·Jesus called out, 'Have you caught anything,
6 friends?' And when they answered, 'No', ·he said,
'Throw the net out to starboard and you'll find something'. So they dropped the net, and there were so many
7 fish that they could not haul it in. ·The disciple Jesus
loved said to Peter, 'It is the Lord'. At these words 'It
is the Lord', Simon Peter, who had practically nothing
on, wrapped his cloak round him and jumped into the
8 water. ·The other disciples came on in the boat, towing
the net and the fish; they were only about a hundred
yards from land.

9 As soon as they came ashore they saw that there was
some bread there, and a charcoal fire with fish cooking
10 on it. ·Jesus said, 'Bring some of the fish you have just
11 caught'. ·Simon Peter went aboard and dragged the net
to the shore, full of big fish, one hundred and fifty-three
of them; and in spite of there being so many the net was
12 not broken. ·Jesus said to them, 'Come and have break-
fast'. None of the disciples was bold enough to ask,
'Who are you?'; they knew quite well it was the Lord.

21 a. Added either by the evangelist or by a disciple of his.

Jesus then stepped forward, took the bread and gave it 13
to them, and the same with the fish. ·This was the third 14
time that Jesus showed himself to the disciples after
rising from the dead.

After the meal Jesus said to Simon Peter, 'Simon son 15
of John, do you love me more than these others do?'
He answered, 'Yes Lord, you know I love you'. Jesus
said to him, 'Feed my lambs'. ·A second time he said 16
to him, 'Simon son of John, do you love me?' He
replied, 'Yes, Lord, you know I love you'. Jesus said
to him, 'Look after my sheep'. ·Then he said to him a 17
third time, 'Simon son of John, do you love me?' Peter
was upset that he asked him the third time, 'Do you
love me?' and said, 'Lord, you know everything; you
know I love you'. Jesus said to him, 'Feed my sheep.

'I tell you most solemnly,   18
when you were young
you put on your own belt
and walked where you liked;
but when you grow old
you will stretch out your hands,
and somebody else will put a belt round you
and take you where you would rather not go.'

In these words he indicated the kind of death by which 19
Peter would give glory to God. After this he said,
'Follow me'.

Peter turned and saw the disciple Jesus loved follow- 20
ing them—the one who had leaned on his breast at the
supper and had said to him, 'Lord, who is it that will
betray you?' ·Seeing him, Peter said to Jesus, 'What 21
about him, Lord?' ·Jesus answered, 'If I want him to 22
stay behind till I come, what does it matter to you?
You are to follow me.' ·The rumour then went out 23

among the brothers that this disciple would not die. Yet Jesus had not said to Peter, 'He will not die', but, 'If I want him to stay behind till I come'.

Conclusion

24 This disciple is the one who vouches for these things and has written them down, and we know that his testimony is true.

25 There were many other things that Jesus did; if all were written down, the world itself, I suppose, would not hold all the books that would have to be written.

NOTES

NOTES

PROLOGUE

Christ is in his own person the Gospel, the Good News. John begins therefore by making clear three points of view from which he must always be considered, and in doing so provides a summary of the teaching contained in the whole work. First, vv. 1–5, he is God the Creator who was 'in the beginning' before the world was made. Second, vv. 6–15, comes the proclamation of the stupendous historical event, the Word was made flesh in the person of Jesus of Nazareth. Third, vv. 16–18, John reflects on the wonder and power of the Risen Christ in the experience of the Church. A distinctive vocabulary is used throughout the gospel and it is important from the outset to remember the special implications of certain words, marked with an asterisk in the following notes, vv. 1–18.

1:1 *In the beginning was the Word.* This is a statement of the pre-existence of Christ, something which St Paul had taught thirty or forty years earlier (Colossians 1:17). The opening is deliberately reminiscent of the creation story (Genesis 1:1). To find out why Christ should be described as 'the Word' we have to go back to the Old Testament.

(i) The word of God had creative force. At the utterance of God, matter came into existence. The gospel will teach that Jesus re-creates humanity.

(ii) The word of God reveals God for what he is, just

as human speech reveals something of the character of the speaker; the beauty of the material world is evidence of the goodness and providence of God. This idea was developed in the experience of the prophets. To them 'the word of the Lord' was a personal revelation, teaching how his nature, purpose, and demands were to be understood from contemporary events. The Gospel is the culmination because Jesus is the perfect revelation of what God is, and does, and requires.

(iii) For any first century Jew 'the word of the Lord' meant particularly the Law. This was primarily to be understood as the record of God's choice of Israel, his covenant relationship with them, and his mighty acts of salvation as described in the Pentateuch, the first five books of the Old Testament. The Gospel is the culmination here as well; the Incarnation and Christ's salvation of the world is the climax of the history of God's dealings with his people. But 'the Law' also meant codes of conduct specifically defined as a measure of obedience to God (Exodus 20:1–17); Jesus summed it up into two commandments, love of God and love of neighbour.

(iv) In the Wisdom Books, the latest strata of literature in the Old Testament, the personified figure of Wisdom (Proverbs 8:22–36) has many of the characteristics earlier associated with 'the Word'. In a remarkable way also, the Law attained near-personification as illustrated for example in Psalm 119. The importance of this lies in the fact that it was the best that feeble man could do to bridge what seemed an intolerable abyss between God and man; it was due to the awareness of the transcendence of God. Jesus, the Word made flesh, is the true link.

For the interpretation which gentiles would put on this first sentence, see Introduction B. (5).

The Word was God. John is quite definite. Jesus

Christ is God (v. 14). It is a point about which some people suppose the New Testament is not precise.

3 *Through him all things came to be.* Christ is the Creator. Notice the emphasis achieved by the negative expression of the same idea in the next line. John was correcting a widely held idea that matter is essentially evil, created by a being who rivalled God both as regards pre-existence and power, a demi-urge as it was called. St Paul found the same error amongst the Colossians and corrected it (Colossians 1:15–16).

4 *All . . . had life* in him.* Material existence has its origin in the Word but John will insist as the gospel develops, that it cannot be compared with the special quality of life described as 'eternal life', bestowed by Jesus and experienced in fellowship with him. There is a distinction between the initial experience of being brought into existence 'through him' and the other type of life which is 'in him'.
That life was the light* of men. God began with the creation of light (Genesis 1:3) and went on to create life in all its forms. The recognition of Jesus as the Son of God precedes the finding of life in him. Light was a common symbol for goodness among the gentiles as among Jews, and we find it too in sayings of Jesus recorded in the synoptic gospels (Mt 5:14–16).

5 *A light that shines in the dark.** Darkness prevailed until God said, 'Let there be light' (Genesis 1:2–3). Christ is the light which reveals the depth of the darkness of evil in the world which cannot overcome him.

6 *A man came, sent by God.* John now considers the event central to human history. John the Baptist had been sent by God to prepare the people for the coming of the Messiah (Mk 1:4–8).

7 *He came as a witness.** In the synoptic gospels the Baptist is represented as a prophet, the last in the line of Old Testament prophets (Mt 11:9). Here his single function is to witness to the fact that Jesus was indeed the Christ so that belief in him might be engendered.

8 *He was not the light.* As in v. 3, a contemporary error is being corrected. By the middle of the first century the Baptist had a huge following, many of whom were ill-instructed and knew nothing of Jesus (Acts 18:24–19:7). It was important to stress his subordinate status.

9 *The Word was the true* light.* John uses the word 'true' as the followers of Plato used it (Introduction B. (5)) to mean 'perfect and original'. The Word is the original and unrefracted light which enlightens all men without distinction. Some catch fire from him and help to overcome the darkness (Mt 5:14–16).

10 *He was in the world.** He came into the world which we live in, the material world, but 'the world' in this gospel also means society hostile to God and it was this which 'did not know him'. 'The world' and 'darkness' mean much the same thing.

11 *His own domain . . . his own people.* The pre-existent Word became a Jew in fulfilment of God's promise to Abraham, the forefather of the Jewish people.

12 *He gave power to become children of God.* We are not children of God simply by virtue of our natural existence. The status is bestowed by him, and continuance and growth made possible by his sustaining power, or grace as it is called (v. 16).
All who believe* in the name. 'To believe' does not mean simply 'to accept as true' certain historical data; it means 'to trust completely'. 'Name' as

elsewhere in the bible stands for the whole personality it refers to, and 'Jesus' means 'God saves'. Those therefore who are in a living relationship of trust in Jesus, receive power to become children of God.

13 *Who was born ... of God himself.* Like Mark, this gospel has no nativity story but John leaves us in no doubt that Jesus had no human father.

14 *The Word was made flesh.* The Word, the Creator, the perfect revelation of the Father (v. 1) was born as man. For gentiles this climax would be questioned as impossible because they thought all matter was evil (v. 3) and would contaminate spirit. To Jews the statement would seem blasphemous although they had always believed that God communicates with men through natural and historical events. For Christians, belief in the Incarnation is the basis of their sacramental practice. Baptism and Holy Communion are the two great sacraments and it is in this gospel that the most important teaching about them is to be found.

He lived among us. In Greek 'he pitched his tent among us'. There is an allusion to the tent which housed the ark of the Lord in the wilderness (Exodus 35:7–11; 40:34–38). The Lord was actually present in the ark. Matter housed Almighty God.

*We saw his glory.** The glory of the Lord always rested over the tent and was a sign of his presence. The glory of Jesus is supremely to be seen in his suffering and death on the cross because it was then that the power of evil was broken (12:32). Whenever the word 'glory' is used in this gospel, it refers to the cost of our salvation in terms of suffering love.

The only Son of the Father. The Son is the perfect revelation of the Father and therefore his suffering and death illustrate the degree to which the Father participates in the experience of his creatures, and the depth of his compassion and mercy (Exodus 34:6). The word 'Son' is not meant to suggest that Christ is secondary to and derived from the Father. It is the best that human language can do to convey that he is of the very essence and being of the Father.

15 *John appears as his witness.* The subordinate status of John the Baptist is again emphasised (vv. 6–8) as we come to the last section of the Prologue, and the significance of the Incarnation to the Church.

16 *From his fullness we have, all of us, received.* The fresh dimension of life experienced as a result of the vital relationship with Christ (v. 12) is described as 'fullness' because it completely satisfies, springing from his 'grace and truth' (v. 14).
Grace in return for grace. Grace is the power of God working in us for our salvation. As we respond to his initial gift, more is given to make the response more complete, the initiative always being on his side because he is the source.

17 *The Law was given through Moses.* The Law which laid down the rules of conduct acceptable to God, was inadequate by itself though it laid the necessary foundation for the demands of Christ and his gifts. The comparison between Moses and the Law on the one hand and Christ and his free gift of salvation on the other is one of the basic themes of the gospel and one which runs right through the New Testament.

18 *No one has ever seen God; it is the only Son . . . who has made him known.* The Prologue concludes with a re-statement of its main point; Jesus Christ is the perfect revelation of God.

I. THE FIRST PASSOVER

A. THE OPENING WEEK

See Introduction D.

In the section which immediately follows (1:19–2:12), chronological notes to be found at 1:29, 35, 43, 2:1 mark the passage of time. By the Jews, seven was regarded as the perfect number, and the climax comes on the seventh day with the miracle at Cana, the first of the 'signs'. Witness is an important theme running through the whole gospel and it is introduced here with the witness of the Baptist and of individual disciples as they respond to the call of Jesus. For its conclusion see 20:24–31. For the importance of witness in the life of the Church see Acts 1:11; Mt 28:19–20. In Greek the word for witness is 'martyr' and it was well understood by the time John wrote that 'the blood of the martyrs is the seed of the Church'.

The witness of John

19 *The Jews sent priests and Levites.* Reference to 'the Jews' as if the writer were not one of them, is characteristic of Jn. The point being made is that from the outset 'his own people' (v. 11) mustered against Jesus. Here the object was to find out about the Baptist's activities whereas in Mt (Mt 3:7), Sadducees (members of priestly families) and Pharisees went to him for baptism. The priests were the aristocrats of Jerusalem and it is curious therefore to hear of their being dispatched by the unidentified group simply described as 'the Jews'. The detail suggests that the writer was out of touch with

conditions in Jerusalem. The Levites were Temple servants.

20 *I am not the Christ.* The inferiority of the Baptist is emphasised from the beginning (v. 8). 'Christ' is the Greek translation of the Hebrew word 'Messiah', the 'Anointed One'. The Jews looked for the coming of a great Priest-King who would deliver them from Roman rule and make their nation and religion supreme.

21 *Are you Elijah? I am not.* A second negative reply emphasising the intention to portray the Baptist solely as witness to Christ. The prophet Malachi had said (Mal 3:23–24) that Elijah would return at the end of history to prepare the people for the coming of the Messiah in judgement, and the establishment of the kingdom of God. In the synoptic gospels the Baptist is said to have fulfilled that role (Mt 17:10–13; Lk 1:16–17) but John disregards the earlier tradition for theological reasons. He will show that judgement and the establishment of the kingdom are not events in the far future, but that they are experienced in the present as individuals accept or reject Christ; it is one of his important themes.
Are you the Prophet? A hope persisted that some new prophet, like Moses, would come to the help of Israel (Deuteronomy 18:15).

23 *I am ... a voice.* The quotation from Isaiah 40:3 sums up everything which John wants to say about the Baptist. It is used by all the synoptists (Mt 3:3; Mk 1:3; Lk 3:4).

24 *These men had been sent by the Pharisees.* (v. 19.) The Pharisees were strongly opposed to the Sadducees and very strict in their observance of the Law. They formed a minority in the Sanhedrin, the Great Council, of which the High Priest was president. See

Mt 23:16–23; Mk 7:1–23 and the commentaries on
the synoptic gospels in this series.

26 *I baptise with water.* (Mk 1:8.) John's baptism was a
sign of repentance for sin (Mt 3:6) and recognised
by him as inadequate (Mt 3:11; Mk 1:8; Lk 3:16;
Jn 1:33).
*There stands among you . . . unknown to you . . . the
one who is coming.* It was believed that the Messiah
would be unknown until he suddenly appeared.

27 *I am not fit to undo his sandal-strap.* (Mt 3:11; Mk
1:7; Lk 3:16.) This was the work of a slave.

28 *Bethany on the other side of Jordan.* This place is not
mentioned in the synoptics and its location is unknown. It is not to be confused with the village on
the Mount of Olives (Mk 11:1; Lk 19:29).

29 *The next day.* The first of the chronological notes
(see the Introduction to this section).
Seeing Jesus coming towards him. Like Mark (Mk
1:9), John expects his readers to know the basic
facts about Jesus and to need no additional explanation as to who he was, and where he came from.
John said, 'Look'. The Word who was God (v. 1) and
made flesh (v. 14) is known as Jesus, 'God saves'.
Through the witness of the Baptist, readers are being
invited to consider more closely the saving work of
Christ.
The lamb of God. In the whole of the New Testament
this strange title is only to be found here, at v. 36,
in I Peter 1:19, and in the Book of Revelation. (i) It
derives from Isaiah 53:7, the last of the poems in
Isaiah often called the Suffering Servant Songs (Is
42:1–9; 49:1–6; 50:4–11; 52:13–53:12). The main
idea is that undeserved suffering endured patiently
by the Servant, creates goodness in the onlookers
because they are moved to gentleness and change of

heart. (ii) 'The lamb' would in Jewish minds immediately be associated with the passover (Exodus
12:3–11), the annual feast commemorating God's
mighty act of salvation. The lamb was an essential
element of the feast and, cooked whole, symbolised
the unity of the people with one another and with
God. The idea that Christ was the true Passover was
already rooted in the tradition when this gospel was
written (I Corinthians 5:7, probably to be dated
about 57).

That takes away the sin of the world. The reference
here is to a ritual distinct from the Passover. On the
Day of Atonement (at-one-ment), Israel fasted and
did penance for the sin which made a barrier between
them and God (Leviticus 16). Animal sacrifice was
offered to remove the guilt of sins committed in
ignorance, the blood representing the life of the man
making the offering. But there was no means of
removing the guilt of deliberate sin. Now through
Christ, God has himself provided the means of doing
away with all sin both deliberate and done in
ignorance, and made possible the reconciliation of
all mankind with himself. In Jewish thinking, blood
was actual life, so 'the blood of Christ' always means
the totality of his self-offering to God. How this
'takes away sin' has already been suggested (v. 12),
and will become clearer as the gospel proceeds.

He existed before me. Not 'he is older'; Christ was
'in the beginning' (v. 1), before all things.

31 *I did not know him myself.* The Baptist did not know
that Jesus was the Messiah until he had received a
special revelation (v. 33).

32 *I saw the Spirit coming down on him.* In the other
gospels Jesus is said to have been baptised by John
the Baptist (Mt 3:13–17; Mk 1:9–11; Lk 3:21–22).
Here characteristically (vv. 20–23), John only saw,

and bore witness. The descent of the Spirit was the anointing of Jesus with the Spirit to the office of Messiah. Both priests and kings were anointed in ancient Israel and the gospel will show that Jesus, priest and victim, reigns from the cross (12:32–33).

Like a dove. The origin of this symbol is uncertain. It probably arose from traditional exposition and interpretation of the creation story (Genesis 1:2), where it is said that God's spirit 'hovered over the water'.

And resting on him. The importance of this point is brought out near the conclusion of his speech. Always filled with the Holy Spirit, Jesus baptises with the Holy Spirit and bestows the Holy Spirit (20:22), giving what the Baptist could not (v. 26).

34 *He is the Chosen One of God.* This recalls the words of the voice from heaven Mk 1:11, 'You are my Son, the Beloved', reminiscent of Isaiah 42:1, the first of the Servant Songs (v. 29 (i)). The Baptist thus bore witness to the fact that Jesus was the expected Messiah.

The first disciples

According to the synoptic gospels, the first disciples were called by the lake of Galilee and there is no suggestion that they had previously been followers of the Baptist (Mk 1:16–20; Mt 4:18–22; Lk 5:1–11). Attempts have been made to harmonise the two accounts but it is probably better simply to accept the fact that there were different traditions. Many of the disciples of the Baptist certainly found their way to Jesus eventually (Acts 18:24–19:7).

35 *On the following day.* Another mention of the passage of time (v. 29). The Baptist again bore witness to what he knew with the immediate result that two of his disciples went after Jesus.

111

38 *Rabbi ... where do you live?* The use of the title
'rabbi' (teacher) shows that they had not understood
what the Baptist had meant. But we have here one of
the double references characteristic of this gospel
(Introduction D.). The real dwelling place of Jesus
is in heaven with the Father. From the beginning to
the present day, discipleship means keeping with him
and so learning about where he belongs, his home.

39 *It was about the tenth hour.* The day was reckoned
from dawn, about 6 a.m., so it was about four o'clock
in the afternoon. It is impossible to say if the detail
is personal reminiscence or whether symbolism,
obvious to the first readers of the gospel, was
intended. It is characteristic of John to mention the
passage of time, and twice more he specifies the hour
(4:6; 19:14).

40 *One of these two ... was Andrew.* In the synoptic
gospels, Andrew's name occurs only in the story of
his call (Mt 4:18–19; Mk 1:16–17), and in the lists
of the Twelve. In Jn he is mentioned on two other
occasions besides this one (6:8–9; 12:20–22).

41 *We have found the Messiah.* In the synoptic gospels
the fact that Jesus was the Messiah was a secret until
Peter's recognition at Caesarea Philippi, the climax
of their account of the ministry (Mt 16:13–20; Mk
8:27–38; Lk 9:18–22). In Jn there is no secret and
recognition comes from the outset. Like the Baptist,
having seen, Andrew bears witness.

42 *You are to be called Cephas.* (Mt 16:17–18.) 'Cephas'
is the Aramaic for 'Rock', Aramaic being the
language in common use in first-century Palestine.
The scriptures were written in Hebrew, and the
services in the Temple and synagogues were in
Hebrew, but teaching was in Aramaic because it was
the language of the people. Apart from this context,

the Aramaic 'Cephas' is to be found only in some of
St Paul's letters (I Corinthians 1:12; 3:22; Galatians
1:18), 'Peter' is the Greek form.

43 *The next day.* See vv. 29, 35.
Jesus had decided to leave for Galilee. Bethany (v. 29)
was on the east side of the river Jordan evidently.
He would have to cross the river to get to Galilee.
He met Philip. Philip is mentioned in the story of the
feeding of the five thousand (6:5–9) and again at
12:20–22. In the synoptic gospels his name only
occurs in the lists of the Twelve. Philip and Andrew
are both Greek names.

44 *Bethsaida.* This was in Galilee, at the north end of the
lake. According to the synoptic tradition, Andrew
and Peter belonged to Capernaum.
Philip found Nathanael. The process of witness, and
the gathering of people round Jesus continues. The
name Nathanael means 'God gives'; he is perhaps
an example of those to whom God gives power to
become his children (v. 12). His name occurs at
21:2 and nowhere else in the New Testament but is
sometimes identified with Bartholomew, one of the
Twelve (Mt 10:3).
The one whom Moses wrote about in the Law. Moses
was believed to have written the whole of the
Pentateuch or Law, the first five books of the Old
Testament. There is no clear reference in them to the
Messiah though his coming has been understood as
implied in the promise given to Abraham (Genesis
12:1–3).
He is Jesus the son of Joseph. It has been already
made quite clear that Jesus was not the son of Joseph.
Jesus was a real historical person and Philip was telling
as much about him as was generally known.

46 *From Nazareth? . . . Can anything good come from*

that place? It is not known why Nazareth should
have had such a reputation. There may have been a
proverbial saying behind the question.

47 *There is an Israelite ... incapable of deceit.* Jacob
acquired the birthright from his brother Esau by a
trick (Genesis 25:28–34) and later the special blessing
of his father Isaac (Genesis 27). He was re-named
when after his struggle with the angel, he became a
reformed character; he was thenceforth Israel
(Genesis 32:22–32) as his descendants, God's
"consecrated nation", would also be known.

48 *I saw you under the fig tree.* The supernatural knowledge of Jesus is brought out from the beginning in
this gospel in contrast to the other three where it is
not emphasised. He knew the character of the man as
well as of his meditation. The pious Israelite was
likely to have as his subject of meditation, the
establishment of the kingdom of God. The next
words suggest as much.

49 *Rabbi, you are the Son of God, you are king of Israel.*
The double title emphasises the strength of Nathanael's conviction; 'Teacher, you are indeed the
Messiah'. As representative of reformed Israel (v. 47)
he hails Jesus as king of all those who having accepted
him (v. 12), are given power to become the children
of God. The idea that the Church is the New Israel
runs through the New Testament, and lies behind
this passage (I Peter 2:9; Exodus 19:5).

51 *You will see the heaven laid open ...* The first verb
is in the plural. Jesus is speaking not only to those
present but to the Church of the future (v. 38). The
words recall the story of Jacob's dream of the ladder
going up to heaven, and the angels ascending and
descending. God was at the top and renewed the
promise first given to Abraham (Genesis 28:10–17;

114

12:1–3). Jesus the Incarnate Son links man to God as Jacob's ladder linked earth and heaven. It is another way of saying what has already been suggested by the title 'lamb of God'; Jesus is the centre of unity as disciples gather round him, and he makes man at one with God (v. 29).

The Son of Man. Nathanael salutes Jesus as Son of God. He is perfect God and perfect man, but the title Son of Man had a special meaning for Jews. The prophet Daniel had a vision and saw:—

> coming on the clouds of heaven,
> one like a son of man.
> . . . . .
> On him was conferred sovereignty,
> glory and kingship,
> and men of all peoples, nations and languages
> became his servants.
>
> (Daniel 7:13–14; Mk 14:62)

The wedding at Cana

This is the first of the signs (Introduction D., E.). The tradition was probably enriched with symbolism before ever it reached John. The story is the witness of first-century Christians to the power of the Risen Christ and has therefore a depth of meaning it would never have if it was only about the transformation of water into wine.

2:1 *Three days later.* Seven was a perfect number and this being the seventh day (1:29), it is of particular importance. And the mention of three days would make any Christian immediately think of the resurrection.

There was a wedding. There may well have been a wedding at Cana which Jesus attended, but the word had very special associations for people brought up in Judaism. The banquet which they believed would inaugurate the kingdom of God after the Messiah had come was often described as a wedding feast as in Mt 22:1–13; 25:1–13. The introduction to the story then, points to the situation of the post-resurrection Church.

The mother of Jesus was there. She is mentioned again in the story of the crucifixion (19:25–27), but her name is never given. Behind the factual statement lies symbolism. She can be held to represent the Judaism from which Jesus took his humanity, aware of the inadequacy of the established religion; there can be no feasting without wine.

4 *Woman, why turn to me?* The form of address was respectful Jewish usage but the question suggests a sharp distinction between Jesus and his mother. See Mk. 1:24.

My hour.* The words belong to the special vocabulary of the gospel. The hour of Christ is equivalent to his glory (1:14). His suffering on the cross was the time of his fullest manifestation.

5 *The servants.* The word is not the usual one in Greek for domestic servants, but 'diaconoi'—the deacons whose function it was to distribute the bread and wine at the Eucharist (Holy Communion). A comparison is being invited between the sterile Jewish expectation of the messianic banquet some time in the far future, and the 'fullness' (1:16) which is the gift of Christ here and now.

Do whatever he tells you. The mother of Jesus stands at the divide. She represents the Israel into which the Incarnate Word was born and also because she is the mother of the Lord, she represents the Church which is the mother of us all. Here she is the Church urging upon her children the duty of absolute obedience.

6 *Six stone jars.* The fact that there were less than

seven, the perfect number, suggests the inadequacy of Jewish rites of purification which cleansed the body but left impurity of heart and mind untouched (Mk 7:1–23).

Each could hold twenty or thirty gallons. A prodigious quantity of wine was to be provided. At the Eucharist, the banquet presided over by Christ the true bridegroom, the guests find cleansing and life such as Judaism cannot possibly provide, and in limitless measure.

9 *The steward.* In a real situation he could not have failed to know what had happened. He perhaps represents the religious authorities responsible for the proper observance of rites and ceremonies, and consistently hostile to Jesus in this gospel (1:19).

11 *He let his glory be seen.* For the meaning of 'glory' see 1:14. It was only after the resurrection that it really came to be understood.

12 *Capernaum.* The home of Peter, James, and John according to the synoptists (1:44; Mk 1:29).

B. The Passover

The cleansing of the Temple (Mt 21:12–13; Mk 11:11, 15–17; Lk 19:45–46)

In the synoptic accounts the cleansing of the Temple took place at the beginning of the last week of the ministry of Jesus, and led immediately to his arrest and crucifixion. In Jn it is placed at the beginning of the ministry either because an independent tradition was used or for theological reasons. It is unlikely that Jesus cleansed the Temple on two occasions. As it stands the story suggests a comparison, like the miracle at Cana, between the old way of salvation provided by Judaism and the new given by Jesus. It is helpful therefore to know something about the importance of the Temple to the Jews.

(1) The Temple. The Temple was holy because it was regarded as the dwelling-place of God. It was realised that he was not confined there and could be approached anywhere, but nevertheless his presence was to be experienced in the Temple particularly. Because God dwelt there, the Temple was unique and there could not be another. It was forbidden to offer sacrifice except in the Temple.

(2) Sacrifice. Worship in the Temple was expressed primarily by sacrifice. Modern usage has led us into the mistake of thinking of this in terms of destruction and loss but it was in fact an offering. Offerings were made in thanksgiving for the fertility of the flocks and fields, a substitute being offered for the first-born son (Lk 2:22–24). Offerings were also made as an expiation for sin. It was believed that blood was life and thus the worshipper offered life to the Giver of life, the blood of the animal representing the total dedication of the man making the offering (1:29).

13 *The Jewish Passover.* So described because for John, Easter—the Christian Passover—had taken its place. *Jesus went up to Jerusalem.* All male Jews were in duty bound to go to Jerusalem for the feast. The Incarnate Son conformed.

14 *People selling cattle and sheep and pigeons.* Sacrificial animals might only be bought within the Temple precincts. The Court of the Gentiles, the only part where gentiles were allowed, was used for this purpose.
The money changers. Purchases had to be paid for with the special Temple currency and it was necessary therefore to change the Roman coinage in normal use. The money changers made their profit.

15 *Making a whip ... knocked their tables over.* The
prophet Malachi (3:1–4) had said that on the Day
of the Lord, when history reached its end and the
rule of God was established, he would come suddenly
in judgement to his Temple.

16 *Take all this out of here.* The Temple was destroyed
and animal sacrifices had come to an end by the time
that John wrote. Jesus was himself the last and
perfect sacrifice, and the only worship offered was
'in spirit and in truth' (4:24).
Stop turning my Father's house into a market. Mk
11:7 quotes Jeremiah 7:11, 'You have made it a den
of robbers'.

17 *His disciples remembered.* Later on we are told that
Jesus promised his disciples that the Holy Spirit
would teach them and remind them of what he had
said (14:26). This process is to be seen at work here.
Zeal for your house will devour you. (Psalm 69:9.)
The psalm describes the anguish of a man persecuted
for his devotion to God and the Temple and so
foreshadows the Passion (the suffering and death of
Jesus).

18 *The Jews intervened.* The priests who were responsible
for the Temple had had their authority challenged by
the action of Jesus. They were 'his own people'
(1:11) but unable to grasp the significance of what
he did and said.
What sign can you show us ... ? The word 'sign' is
used here in the ordinary sense. They wanted to see
something spectacular which they could accept as
proof of his right to act with authority (Mt 12:38;
Lk 11:29).

19 *Destroy this sanctuary ...* The resurrection is the
one sign that will be given vv. 21–22 (Mt 12:39–40;
Lk 11:29–30). The synoptic gospels report that false

119

witnesses charged Jesus with saying this (Mt 26:61; Mk 12:58) but they have no record of his actually saying it though he did prophesy the destruction of the Temple (Mk 13:1).

20 *It has taken forty-six years to build.* This very interesting detail may be a valuable piece of reminiscence. King Herod the Great began the reconstruction of the Temple in 19 B.C. and this would then be the passover of A.D. 28. The Temple was completed in 63, only seven years before its destruction by the Romans.

21 *The sanctuary that was his body.* The human body of Jesus which he took from Mary his mother was raised from the dead on the third day. The Holy Spirit was poured forth upon the believing disciples fifty days later, uniting them into the body of Christ ... his Church created to continue his work in the world (I Corinthians 12:12–31; Ephesians 4:11–15).

22 *His disciples remembered.* See v. 17.

They believed the scripture. Probably not any particular passage but the Old Testament as a whole, foreshadowing the salvation which is in Christ.

24 *Jesus knew them all.* Jesus had known all about Nathanael when he saw him coming. His divine insight is now reaffirmed.

C. THE MYSTERY OF THE SPIRIT REVEALED TO A MASTER IN ISRAEL

The conversation with Nicodemus

The story of the cleansing of the Temple shows Jesus as the fulfilment of all that the sacrificial system of

Judaism strove to achieve, especially in relation to the priestly party, the Sadducees, who were responsible for the system. Now he is to be shown in relation to the Pharisees, the rival group whose special sphere of influence was in the synagogues which provided the non-sacrificial element in Jewish worship. Synagogue worship had developed during the Jewish exile in Babylon in the 6th century B.C. to compensate for the loss of the Temple and its rites. By the time the gospel was written, the Temple had been destroyed (2:20) and the synagogues alone had to provide for the religious needs of the people. In the poetic passages which follow, Jesus is talking in two ways. In his Incarnate life he helps the puzzled Pharisee; later through the Church which is his body he speaks as it bears witness to its experience of the power of the Holy Spirit, indwelling, directing, and teaching it. It is not possible always to be exact and to say at which point Jesus is talking to Nicodemus and when the Church is his mouthpiece, but this does not matter. We can be sure that we have his authentic voice.

3:1 *Nicodemus.* His name occurs twice more in this gospel (7:45–52; 19:39) but nowhere else in the New Testament. Described as 'a leading Jew', we should infer that he was a member of the Sanhedrin, the Great Council responsible for Jewish affairs to the Roman Governor.

2 *(He) came to Jesus by night.* This can be understood literally as a wise precaution in view of what had taken place in the Temple. But at the same time he must be recognised as one who had seen the signs (2:23) and been attracted out of the darkness to 'the light of men' (1:4).
We know that you are a teacher come from God. Unlike the disciples and Nathanael (1:41, 45, 49)

121

he was unable to see beyond that. He did not ask a question but there was no need to. Jesus knew what was in his mind.

3 *Unless a man is born from above* ... The unasked question seems to have been that of the rich young man (Mk 10:17), and the lawyer (Lk 10:25): 'What must I do to inherit eternal life?' It is not what a man can do but what happens to him. A heavenly be-getting is the essential preliminary for being born anew.

He cannot see the kingdom of God. The kingdom of God was the old Jewish term for what was believed would happen at the end of time. All men would have to stand before the judgement throne of God and then his rule would be established for ever (1:21). The idea was one which Nicodemus had accepted all his life.

4 *How can a grown man be born?* The Jews are always represented in this gospel as interpreting the words of Jesus in their most literal sense (2:20).

Unless a man is born through water and the Spirit. The Baptist had seen the Spirit coming down and resting upon Jesus (1:32) and knew that he would baptise with the Holy Spirit. This then is a reference to baptism, the first essential sacrament of the Church (1:14). A sacrament is 'an outward and visible sign of an inward and spiritual grace given to us'. The water of baptism which is 'the outward and visible sign' conveys spiritual cleansing; it also conveys a life completely distinct from ordinary natural life—the Holy Spirit himself is given. Baptism is then a once for all experience which cannot be repeated any more than natural birth.

6 *What is born of the Spirit is spirit.* The point is not that the flesh is a lower mode of life and the spirit a

higher, but simply that there are two quite different
kinds or dimensions of life.

8 *The wind blows wherever it pleases.* In the original
there is a play on words which cannot be reproduced
in English. In Greek 'pneuma' means both 'wind'
and 'spirit'. Their activity is alike strong, life-giving,
unpredictable.

11 *We speak only about what we know.* This seems to be
Christ speaking through his Church as it bears
witness to experience.

12 *Things in this world ... heavenly things.* Spiritual
truth can only be conveyed by metaphor and parable.

13 *No one has gone up to heaven. ...* A reference to the
ascension of Jesus, when he returned to the Father
after the resurrection and appeared no more to his
disciples.
The Son of Man who is in heaven. Jesus is the link
between God and man (2:51) because he shares
both the divine and human natures, and because he
is the Redeemer of men (1:29).

14 *The Son of Man must be lifted up.* The lifting up of
the Son of Man always refers to the different aspects
of his unique glory; his suffering on the cross, his
resurrection from the dead, and his ascension to the
Father in heaven.
As Moses lifted up the serpent in the desert. (Numbers
24:4–9.) Israel rebelled against God then prayed to
him for help when smitten by a plague of fiery
serpents as a punishment. Moses was told by God
to make a bronze serpent and put it on a standard,
and then when the people looked at it they were
healed from the bites of the serpents.

15 *So that everyone who believes may have eternal life.*
Here is the answer to Nicodemus's problem. Every-

one who trusts in the saving power of Jesus 'lifted up' (v. 14) may enjoy in the present that other kind or dimension of life (vv. 5–6) described here as 'eternal life', and in the Jewish phraseology as 'seeing the kingdom of God' (v. 3).

16 *God loved the world so much* ... The love of God embraces all mankind and is not limited to one people. He loved so much that he gave all he had, his only Son.
That everyone who believes in him may not be lost. Everyone is included in God's love, but eternal life cannot be experienced apart from trust in Jesus.

18 *Whoever refuses to believe is condemned already.* It is not God who condemns. The man who refuses to believe deprives himself of eternal life.
He has refused to believe in the name of God's only Son. He has refused to put his whole trust in Jesus. For the force of the expression 'to believe in the name', see 1:12.

19 *On these grounds is sentence pronounced.* This is a re-interpretation of the Jewish concept of judgement and the establishment of the kingdom of God (1:21; 3:3). Judgement takes place in this life as men accept or reject Christ and 'enter the kingdom of God' (v. 3) or not (vv. 15–16).
Light is come into the world. See 1:4–5.

21 *The man who lives by the truth.* I.e. 'He listens to the voice of Jesus' (18:37); he obeys him (2:5).

II. JOURNEYS IN SAMARIA AND GALILEE

John bears witness for the last time

22 *Jesus ... baptised.* Nowhere else in the gospels is

there mention of Jesus baptising, and according to
the synoptic tradition he did not begin his ministry
until the Baptist's imprisonment (Mk 1:14). See also
Mt 11:2–11; Mk 6:17–29.

23 *Aenon near Salem.* Only mentioned in this gospel. It
was no doubt in the Jordan valley, but where is not
known.

25 *A discussion with a Jew about baptism.* What follows
seems to have been intended as a summing up of
what has already been said about the Baptist as
compared with Jesus, and the adequacy of the two
baptisms. It may well have been a subject much under
discussion at Ephesus or wherever it was that the
gospel was written.

29 *The bride is only for the bridegroom.* The idea derives
from the Old Testament where Yahweh is often
described as the husband of Israel. It passed into the
New Testament with sayings and parables of Jesus
in which he identifies himself with the bridegroom
(Mk 2:19–20; Mt 25:1–13).

30 *I must grow smaller.* He was only a witness (1:7);
he was not the light (1:8); he was only a voice in the
wilderness (1:23); his baptism was only water
baptism (1:33).

31 *He who comes from heaven bears witness.* This is an
aspect of the subject of witness which will be developed later. It is not only that the disciples and the
later Church bear witness to Christ; Christ himself
bears witness to the Father.

36 *Anyone who believes . . . anyone who refuses to believe.*
The alternatives are as stark in the gospel as they are
in the Old Testament; there is a way of life and a
way of death (Deuteronomy 30:15–20).

The anger of God. As in the Old Testament, this phrase is not intended to suggest that God experiences hostile emotion which he vents on the disobedient. But the life of the flesh and of the spirit (3:6) both originate from him and disregard of what is necessary for their continuance can have only one result: loss.

The saviour of the world revealed to the Samaritans

Jesus has been shown in relationship with the Sadducees and Pharisees, the two great parties of Judaism. Now he is to be revealed to the Samaritans, despised by all orthodox Jews on both racial and religious grounds. In the 8th century B.C. the northern part of what had once been David's kingdom was conquered by the Assyrians under Sennacherib. A large proportion of the population was deported, foreigners being brought in as colonists. The newcomers were heathen but though they adopted the religion of Yahweh (2 Kings 17:24–41), they were never accepted as brethren by the Jews of Judaea. In the 2nd century B.C. the hostility between the orthodox and the Samaritans came to a head, the Samaritans severing all relationship by building their own Temple on Mount Gerizim, and maintaining that it was there and not in Jerusalem that the only legitimate sacrifices might be offered. The schism occurred after the Pentateuch (the first five books of the Old Testament) had assumed its final form and that remained the one thing that the orthodox and the Samaritans had in common. The story of the woman at the well occurs only in Jn, and Lk is the only synoptic gospel to make any mention at all of the Samaritans (Lk 9:51–56; 10:30–37; 17:11–19). See also Acts 8:4–25.

4:4 *He had to cross Samaria.* It was the most direct and convenient route but because of the Samaritans' hostility, was avoided by many Jews.

5 *Sychar.* This is usually identified with a village called Askar at the foot of Mt Ebal. A well nearby seems always to have been called Jacob's Well though it is not mentioned in Genesis.

6 *Jesus, tired by the journey, sat.* John who always emphasises the divinity of our Lord, underlines too the reality of the human limitations he suffered. We are probably intended to infer that his weariness was more than physical as he considered the inadequacy of Judaism as typified by the well (2:1–10; 13–22).
It was about the sixth hour. Reckoning from sunrise (1:39) it was about noon. Throughout the story there is a subtle parallel with the Passion Narrative which is worth following if only because it illustrates John's faculty for seeing a pattern in events. It was at that hour that 'his own people' (1:11) utterly rejected him as they told Pilate, 'We have no king but Caesar' (19:14–15). But their rejection and the cross led to the salvation of the world. At the end of this story the Samaritans recognised him as 'saviour of the world' (v. 42).

7 *A Samaritan woman came to draw water.* It was strange to come in the heat of the day. The early morning and the evening were the usual times.
Water. Water is an important symbol in this gospel. We have already seen it as a symbol of cleansing in the baptism of John the Baptist. In the Old Testament it often stands for the never failing mercy and saving help of God, and then by natural extension for life, the kind of life that is 'born through water and the Spirit' (3:5). The literature was after all the product of a people that knew only too well that water is a

basic necessity for the maintenance of physical existence.

Give me a drink. Only in Jn do we have the words of Jesus on the cross, 'I am thirsty' (19:28). It was not only the terrible physical thirst, but the longing to bestow salvation. There is a saying in Lk which suggests the pain he suffered from his human limitations (Lk 12:49–50).

9 *You are a Jew and you ask me, a Samaritan, for a drink?* Contact with a Samaritan meant defilement for any orthodox Jew and in any case it was contrary to Jewish custom for a man to speak to a woman outside the family circle. Jesus was reaching out to humanity in its least respected form.

11 *Living water.* In the literal sense this is water gushing from a spring as opposed to stagnant water that has seeped into a cistern or well.

You have no bucket, sir. She took the words of Jesus at their face value (2:20; 3:4).

12 *Our father Jacob who gave us this well.* The Samaritans claimed to be true Israelites, descendants of Jacob.

14 *The water that I shall give.* The prophet Ezekiel had a vision of a wonderful rushing stream that welled up in the Temple and flowing outwards from it, made the land on both banks rich in vegetation (Ezekiel 47:1–12). Jesus had told the Jews in the Temple, 'Destroy this sanctuary, and in three days I will raise it' (2:19), and we are told that he spoke of the sanctuary that was his body (2:20–22). Only in this gospel do we hear of his pierced side and the flow of blood and water (19:34).

16 *Go and call your husband.* The change of subject seems abrupt but she may have understood that Jesus was telling her to consider the truth and reality

of the gods she customarily worshipped. Throughout the Middle East it was usual to describe gods as husbands of their worshippers (3:29). There were five false gods worshipped by Samaritans.

18 *You have had five.* Her marital experience was paralleled by her religious practice.

19 *I see you are a prophet.* She appears to have seen Jesus's double meaning and like Nathanael (1:49–50) shows her increasing respect by the titles she gives him.

20 *This mountain.* Mount Gerizim. See the introductory note to this chapter.

21 *Neither on this mountain nor in Jerusalem.* After the fall of Jerusalem and the destruction of the Temple in A.D. 70, Jewish worship would be centred in the synagogues and Christian worship would be in and through Jesus (2:19–21; 4:14).

22 *You worship what you do not know.* By breaking away from orthodox Judaism the Samaritans had placed themselves outside the mainstream of revelation. Their worship of the true God was ignorant and deficient.

23 *But the hour will come* ... There were already true worshippers as disciples saw Jesus and believed. After the resurrection there would be many more.
In spirit and truth. Born of water and the Spirit (3:5) and living 'by the truth' in obedience to Jesus (3:21), the worshipper offers himself entire to the Father. His whole life is given to God.

25 *I know that Messiah ... is coming.* When the Messiah came to establish the kingdom of God he would teach the people about worship.

26 *I am he.* (1:41.) Only in this gospel does Jesus say plainly that he is the Messiah, and then to someone

who was a rank outsider (v. 9). Very important here is the veiled allusion to his divinity which will be repeated on a number of other occasions. Moses was told that the name of the God of his fathers was I AM (Exodus 3:13–15), in Hebrew *Yahweh*, and it was Yahweh himself who revealed it. ('Jehovah' is the faulty 16th-century transliteration of the Hebrew, not then so well understood.)

27 *His disciples were surprised.* See v. 9.

28 *The woman put down her water jar.* It was a symbolic gesture. She no longer needed to draw water from Jacob's well, Judaism, because she knew where to find 'living water'.

33 *Has someone been bringing him food?* The disciples show the same lack of comprehension as the woman (v. 11), Nicodemus (3:4), and the Jews (2:20).

34 *My food is to do the will of the one who sent me.* The story of the agony in the garden is not recorded in Jn, but all through the gospel there is insistence that Jesus had come to do the will of the Father (Mk 14:36).
And to accomplish his work. Only to be found in Jn is the last word of Jesus on the cross, 'It is accomplished' (19:30).

35 *The fields . . . ready for harvest.* (Mt 9:37–38.) In the parable of the sower (Mk 4:8), Jesus foresaw a bumper crop, and in this instance the Samaritans were soon to be harvested.

38 *I sent you to reap a harvest you had not worked for.* This suggests the perspective of the early Church rather than the circumstances of the ministry of Jesus. The apostles built on the foundations laid by the prophets and saints of Old Testament times as well as on the work of each other (I Corinthians 3:10–15).

39 *The woman's testimony.* She also having seen and
believed, bore witness.

42 *We ... believe because ... we have heard him ourselves.* There is a difference between knowing about
Jesus and knowing Jesus. 'To believe' is 'to trust'
and that can only be at first hand.
The saviour of the world. The ideas connected with
the title Messiah were essentially Jewish. The word
'saviour' conveyed infinitely more to first-century
gentiles until 'Christ' came to be accepted as a
personal name by perhaps the majority of believers.
Notice the emphasis on the fact that the Good News
is for all mankind—its universality is stressed by
John (3:16–17). The point is immediately driven
home.

The cure of the nobleman's son (Mt 8:5–13; Lk
7:1–10)

Jesus has been shown with members of the established religion; the Sadducees (2:13–22), Nicodemus
the Pharisee (3:1–21), and with the Samaritans who,
though unaccepted, were on the fringe. Now in the
story of this second sign he is in contact with someone beyond the fringe, a pure gentile.

44 *There is no respect for a prophet in his own country.*
(Mk 6:4; Mt 13:37; Lk 4:24.) In the synoptic
gospels Jesus said this after his rejection at Nazareth
where he grew up. In Jn the words apply to Jerusalem
where he would be put to death.

46 *He went again to Cana ...* This is mentioned perhaps
as a reminder of the richness and overflowing
generosity of Christ's provision, available to gentiles
as well as Jews.
A court official. In the service of Herod Antipas, ruler
of Galilee—not a king though he kept royal state.

Herod employed many gentiles. In Mt and Lk it was a Roman centurion who asked Jesus to heal his servant.

Capernaum. (2:12). Also the scene of the cure in Mt and Lk.

48 *So you will not believe unless you see signs and portents.* Trust had to be in Jesus himself. Miracles were only nine-day wonders unless they were understood as showing who Christ was (2:23–25).

50 *Your son will live.* As in Mt and Lk the healing was immediate and effected from a distance. That is wonder enough at the physical level but the story is told to illustrate the truth of what Jesus had said to Nicodemus: 'Everyone who believes may have eternal life in him' (3:15). Jesus is the source of this fresh kind of life.

52 *The seventh hour.* Seven is the number of perfection (2:1). It was a moment of climax when trust was vindicated.

53 *He and all his household believed.* In the early Church whole households would be converted to Christianity and this was the expression commonly used.

III. THE SECOND FEAST AT JERUSALEM

The cure of a sick man at the Pool of Bethzatha (3rd sign)

5:1 *There was a Jewish festival.* We are not told which it was. Jesus is being shown against the background of Temple observances which he would supersede (2:20–21).

2 *The Sheep Pool.* Water is a continuing theme. The pool did not heal all the time, and was just a desperate

NOTES   5:18

hope for someone not only chronically sick but friendless as well (v. 7). A comparison seems to be implied between the spiritual provision available in Judaism and the 'fullness' (1:16) which is the gift of Christ.

3 *Blind, lame, paralysed.* The prophet Isaiah foretells the healing of such people when the kingdom of God is established (Isaiah 35:5–6). In Lk they have places at the great supper, the New Testament equivalent (Lk 14:15–24).

5 *Thirty-eight years.* Israel had to wait thirty-eight years in the wilderness for the promise of God to be fulfilled (Deuteronomy 2:14). John may have thought of the man as representative of his people.

6 *Jesus saw him . . . and knew . . .* (2:24–25.)

8 *Get up . . . and walk.* The words recall the story of the cure of the paralytic (Mk 2:1–12) but here the healing was not preceded by the forgiveness of sins except by implication (v. 14).

10 *That day happened to be the sabbath.* The synoptic gospels stress the fact that the religious authorities regarded as intolerable the disregard by Jesus of man-made sabbath regulations (Mk 2:23–28; 3:1–6; Lk 13:10–17).

14 *Be sure not to sin any more.* See v. 8.

17 *My Father goes on working, and so do I.* 'God . . . rested on the seventh day after all the work he had been doing' (Genesis 2:2). The rabbis taught that although God ceased from his work of creation on the seventh day, the sabbath, he continued to govern and judge the world. By forgiving sins and exercising authority on the sabbath, Jesus had shared with God in the government of the world.

18 *That only made the Jews more intent on killing him.*

What Jesus had said was blasphemy if it was not true. The penalty for blasphemy was death. See Mk 2:7 where the scribes arrived at the same conclusion.

THE DISCOURSE vv. 19–47: see Introduction D.
The healing just described demonstrated the divine authority of Jesus. The Jews failed to interpret the sign and accused him of blasphemy in making himself God's equal. In the passage which follows, Jesus answers the charge. (i) vv. 19–29. Jesus speaks of his relationship with the Father. Far from being in opposition to God, he is perfectly at one with him. (ii) vv. 30–49. The Jews had no excuse for not recognising that he had been sent from God because of the witnesses who had vouched for him—the Father, the Baptist, his own miracles, the scriptures, and the Law.

19 *The Son can do nothing by himself.* For the word 'Son' see 1:14. This and similar passages have led some people to suppose that the Son is subordinate to the Father and not really God. That is wrong. Because Jesus is God (1:1–3, 14) it is not in his nature to act independently of the Father. The Father and the Son work together for the salvation of the world.

20 *The Father loves the Son and shows him everything.* The Son is perfect man as well as perfect God, and as man fully reveals the Father (14:9).
Even greater things. The man lying chronically sick by the pool had been made whole in body and soul. His physical ability to stand, walk and carry a load typifies his usefulness as a servant of God. Like the nobleman's son he had been rescued from a grave situation. The 'greater things' will be miracles of resurrection.

21 *The Son gives life to anyone he chooses.* 'The secret

of the kingdom of God is given' to some and not all (Mk 3:11). Isaiah had recognised the problem (Isaiah 6:9–11) and St Paul had grappled with it (Romans 9–11).

22 (*The Father*) *has entrusted all judgement to the Son.* (Mt 25:31–46.) The Father is beyond all our capacity to see and comprehend, but the Son took our humanity to show us God within the limits of our perspective. As we respond to the Son therefore, or fail to do so, we find life or death (3:18–19) and thus judgement is said to have been given to the Son.

23 *That all may honour the Son as they honour the Father.* The Son, as man, was 'sent'. The manhood was taken at a certain date in history, the Word who took the manhood being before all time (1:1). The Son, like an ambassador whose function is indicated by the word 'sent', is fully representative of the One from whom he came.

24 *Whoever listens to my words.* Listening carries the implication of assimilation and obedience. Response to the revelation of God in Jesus brings a man out of death into life.

25 *The hour will come . . . it is already here.* The spiritually dead are being raised to life here and now, anticipating the resurrection of the dead at the end of time (v. 28).

26 *The Son the source of life.* 1:3–4; 4:14.

27 (*The Father,*) *because he is the Son of Man, has appointed him supreme judge.* See v. 22. There is a reference here to the Son of Man of Daniel's vision (1:51).

30 *I can do nothing by myself.* Because he is totally at one with the Father, v. 19.

135

31 *Were I to testify on my own behalf* ... We come now to the second part of Jesus's reply to his accusers. In a court of law the testimony of the accused would never be accepted unless it were supported by creditable witnesses.

32 *There is another witness who can speak on my behalf.* Some authorities suggest that this is the Father, others that it is John the Baptist. The Father is mentioned quite plainly at v. 37 and the sequence of thought seems clearer if this is taken as referring to John the Baptist.

33 *You sent messengers to John.* 1:19. John's testimony was based on revelation, 1:32–33.

36 *These same works of mine testify.* The cure of the nobleman's son and of the man at the Pool were not only physical healings. In each case 'life from above' was given.

38 *His word.* For the significance of this see 1:1.

39 *You study the scriptures.* The Old Testament as a whole foreshadows Christ. They should have had the discernment to recognise him.

44 *You look to one another for approval.* People won respect for their care in keeping the oral law, the small rituals which governed every detail of daily life (Mk 7:1–13), often neglecting moral issues.

45 *Moses will be your accuser.* 1:1 (iii). It was believed that Moses had written the whole of the Pentateuch or Law, the first five books of the Old Testament and the most important.

IV. ANOTHER PASSOVER, THE BREAD OF LIFE

The story of the miracle of the loaves, the only synoptic miracle story clearly used by John, is set significantly in the context of the Passover, the commemoration of God's mighty act of salvation (Introduction D). It is immediately followed by the discourse on 'the bread of life' in which Jesus says that his flesh is real food and his blood is real drink. The Eucharist (Holy Communion) was plainly in the forefront of John's mind as he wrote. In his account of the Last Supper however, he makes no mention of the institution of the rite. He may have decided that his readers being perfectly familiar with that, it was better to concentrate on the transmission of teaching about it not to be found elsewhere. Possibly he judged it unwise to make public in a predominantly heathen community, details about the second essential sacrament of the Church (1:14; 3:4). Holy things were for holy people.

The miracle of the loaves (4th sign) (Mt 14:13–21; Mk 6:32–44; Lk 9:10–17)

6:1 *Tiberias.* The fine town of Tiberias on the shores of lake Galilee, named after the emperor, was built by Herod Antipas and not completed until A.D. 28. It was only after the close of the first century that the lake came to be called after it, a detail which has a bearing on the date of the gospel.

3 *Jesus climbed the hillside, and sat down.* As in Mt 5:1 the words are meant to suggest that a greater than Moses had come (Exodus 19, 20). Sitting was the posture of majesty.

4 *The Jewish feast of the Passover.* (2:13.) Another

reminder of its supersession by the Christian Passover (Introduction D).

5 *Jesus ... said ... 'Where can we buy some bread?'*
In the other gospels it is the disciples who said this, but it is characteristic of John to show Jesus as always keeping the initiative. Philip and Andrew (1:40, 43) are not mentioned in the other accounts of the miracle. The inclusion of names is always an indication of a later, not an earlier version, of a story.

6 *He himself knew exactly what he was going to do.* The divine knowledge and authority is again made clear (1:48; 2:24–25; 5:17).

7 *Two hundred denarii.* A denarius was the average daily wage for a working man so this was not the kind of sum Jesus and his disciples were likely to have with them. In Mk the disciples suggested ironically that they should spend that amount.

9 *There is a small boy here.* He appears only in this gospel.
Five barley loaves and two fish. It is only here that we are told that they were barley loaves. The loaves and fish were used as an emblem of the Eucharist in the early Church, as for example in the catacombs in Rome. The drawing of a fish by itself was a secret sign in dangerous times to show that any particular person or family was Christian. The fish was also a reminder of the Christian creed. Each letter of the Greek word 'ichthys' (fish) is the first of the six words, 'Jesus Christ, Son of God, Saviour'.

11 *Jesus took the loaves ... gave thanks, and gave them out.* These are the actions essential in the celebration of the Eucharist (the Greek word for Thanksgiving). The breaking of the bread included by all the synoptists as well as St Paul (I Corinthians 11:24) is omitted here. It points to the self-offering of Jesus

on the cross and John seems to have wanted to present the miracle and therefore the Eucharist, in terms of the Messianic Banquet which would inaugurate the kingdom of God (2:1). As host it is Jesus himself who distributes the food here whereas in the other accounts it is the disciples who do it.

12 *Pick up the pieces left over.* The quantity of the fragments illustrates the abundant generosity of Christ's provision. It was the food that really satisfied just as the wine at the marriage feast at Cana was unsurpassed. But the word used by John for 'picking up' ('synagein', generally describing the gathering together of the congregation) suggests that John was thinking also of the 'other sheep ... not of this fold' (10:16) provided for in the synoptic tradition by the feeding of the four thousand (Mk 8:1–10; Mt 15:32–39), gentiles that is to say.

14 *This really is the prophet who is coming.* (1:21; Deuteronomy 18:15).

15 *Jesus could see they were about to ... make him king.* The people saw the feeding as a sign that Jesus was the Messiah and the attempt to make him king was logical. Again Jesus knew exactly what was happening and events were entirely in his control. For the attitude of Jesus to his vocation as Messiah see Mt 4:1–11; Lk 4:1–12 in the commentaries in this series.

Jesus walks on the waters (Mt 14:22–23; Mk 6:45–52)

The synoptists all tell the story of Jesus calming the storm when crossing the lake with his disciples (Mk 4:35–41) and only Lk omits the related story of Christ walking on the water, considered by most authorities to be an allegorised version of the other. Because of the danger of seafaring in ancient times, the sea became the symbol in literature for disaster.

Here the boat stands for the Church faced with a hostile world. In that situation the presence of Christ is a sure defence.

17 *It was getting dark.* (1:5.) The darkness represents the forces of evil mobilising against the Church.

19 *They saw Jesus walking on the lake.* Attempts have been made to rationalise this statement by suggesting that Jesus was walking on the edge of the lake and that the boat had been blown inshore. The point is that Jesus never forsakes his Church. He is always there (Mt 28:20).
This frightened them. In times of great crisis or tremendous pressure, the individual may become vividly aware of weakness in the face of overwhelming odds. In such a situation there is no help but God, and the realisation of this is frightening.

20 *It is I. Do not be afraid.* See 4:26 for the significance of the first words. God is there as a friend at the heart of the turmoil.

21 *In no time it reached the shore.* The supernatural element is heightened. The presence of Jesus in his Church brings an inner security which hostile external forces cannot touch.

The discourse in the synagogue at Capernaum

The conviction that because God is good he will provide enough food for his people runs through the Old Testament, and because existence was precarious, awareness of dependence on God was articulate. Shortage was understood as a wholesome reminder of this dependence: the manna which fell from heaven to sustain them during the forty years in the wilderness after the escape from Egypt (Exodus 16:14–36) was enough, and no more. The prophets taught that God not only sustains a person's physical life, but his inner being, his 'heart', as well. 'The meadows of green grass' (Psalm 23:2) and 'the rich pastures on the mountains of Israel' (Ezekiel 34:14) represent God's spiritual provision for his people. In Jn this teaching is taken a stage further. Jesus is himself 'the true bread'.

26 *You had all the bread you wanted to eat.* Having benefited by the miracle of the loaves, the people thought they could use Jesus as their instrument against the Romans, and that after victory they could be sure of being adequately fed.

27 *Food that cannot last ... food that endures to eternal life.* Physical life and spiritual life each need their appropriate food; one kind for temporal existence and the other for eternity. It is the latter which is the real necessity (3:5–6; 14–15).
The kind of food the Son of Man is offering you. The title 'Son of Man' (1:51; 3:13–14; 5:27; Mk 14:62) points forward to the suffering and glory (1:14) of Jesus. The 'breaking of bread', the Eucharist, was customary in the Church from the very beginning (Lk 24:30–31; Acts 2:46).
On him, the Father ... has set his seal. The descent of the Spirit upon Jesus (1:33) at the moment of his anointing as Messiah, was the setting of God's seal. In the early Church, baptism was often described as 'being sealed'.

28 *What must we do ... ?* The people saw that material considerations were not to be given priority and supposed that good works of some kind were required.

29 *You must believe in the one he has sent.* It is not a matter of activity of any kind, but of believing and trusting in Jesus (Lk 10:38–42).

30 *What sign will you give ... ?* (Mt 12:38–40.) They

wanted proof that Jesus had been sent by God. They did not understand that 'to believe' meant 'to trust'.

31 *Our fathers had manna to eat in the desert.* (Exodus 16.) They challenge Jesus to do something more wonderful than Moses.
As scripture says . . . Psalm 78:24.

32 *It was not Moses who gave you bread.* It was God not Moses who had provided the manna, and it was material food for the body.
The true bread. For 'true' see 1:9 and Introduction B. (5). The 'true bread' 'endures to eternal life' as contrasted with simple physical life. It also gives life to the whole world and not only to Israelites.

34 *Sir . . . give us that bread always.* Their response was like that of the Samaritan woman (4:15).

35 *I am the bread of life.* (4:26; 6:20.) The Incarnate Word, come down from heaven (33) is the true bread which gives life to the world.
He who comes . . . he who believes. The 'coming' and 'believing' are the same. It is the approach of 'the little children' (Mk 10:14) to whom the kingdom of God belongs.

36 *You can see me and still you do not believe.* They see but make nothing of what they see (Mk 4:12).

38 *I have come . . . not to do my own will.* There is perfect unity as between the Father and the Son (5:19–20).

40 *Whoever sees the Son.* Whoever understands and acknowledges that the Son has been sent by the Father.
I shall raise him up on the last day. To trust in Jesus is to be in relationship with him, born into a life (3:5) which physical death does not extinguish.

41 *The Jews were complaining.* As their forefathers

complained against Moses in the wilderness (Exodus 16:2f).

42 *Surely this is Jesus son of Joseph.* (1:45.) Like the people of Nazareth (Mk 6:1-6; Lk 4:16-30) they could not see Jesus as he really was because they thought they knew all about him. It was commonly supposed that when the Messiah came, his origin would be a mystery.

45 *They will all be taught by God.* (Jeremiah 31:35; Isaiah 54:13.) The ingathering of people to Jesus as they responded to the will of the Father was a process the prophets had written about, as the Jews should recognise. It was useless to complain because their preconceived ideas were challenged.

46 *Not that anybody has seen the Father.* More than physical sight is meant. Only Jesus has first-hand knowledge of the Father. 'God is hidden' (Isaiah 45:15).

50 *That a man may eat it and not die.* The certainty of physical death is not in question. It is that other life, born of water and the Spirit (3:5) and nourished by the bread of life, which will not die (v. 40).

51 *The bread that I shall give is my flesh.* We are told in the Prologue that the Word was made flesh; people of first-century Palestine met and listened to Jesus, a man with a body like the rest of us. Since the resurrection he is encountered differently. First, the Church, 'the company of all faithful people', is his body doing his work in the world. Second, at the Last Supper before his arrest and crucifixion he instituted the Eucharist (Holy Communion) (Mk 14:22-25) where his presence is particularly to be found and where, in the sacramental bread and wine, his body and blood (his life) are taken and received by faith. The Eucharist is the true Passover uniting

God and man, and men with one another. (See the note on The Lamb of God (ii) at 1:29.)

My flesh for the life of the world. Introduced by the miracle of the loaves, the banquet which inaugurates the kingdom of God (2:1; 6:14), the emphasis has been on the food and eating it. This now shifts to the cost to Christ in making the food available for the whole world, and the language is sacrificial. (See the note on sacrifice preceding 2:13–22.) The sin offerings of the Old Dispensation were the best that men could do to remove the guilt of sin, but inadequate. In Jesus, God has himself provided the perfect and effective offering. The word 'flesh' is inclusive of his whole personality, cleansing from sin and infusing with life.

52 *How can this man give us his flesh to eat?* It is the natural question of outsiders and one, no doubt, which John had frequently heard. It is typical of 'the Jews' as they are portrayed in this gospel.

53 *If you do not eat the flesh of the Son of Man.* (v. 27.) The words look forward to the time after his resurrection and ascension when he can only be known in his body the Church, and particularly in the Eucharist. Sharing in his death on the cross by dying to sin and self is essential to the eating (the assimilation) of his 'flesh'.

And drink his blood. It will be remembered that the Jews thought that blood was actually life. (See the note on Sacrifice introducing 2:13–25.) The life born of the Spirit (3:5) needs to be nourished by the very life of Christ, by its nature 'eternal' (Romans 6:8–11).

56 *He . . . lives in me and I live in him.* (15:4–5.) Christ working in our minds and wills is Christ 'within us'. Our individual and corporate response to him in the Church is living 'in' him. St Paul understood growth

in the Christian life in the same way (Galatians 2:20; 4:19).

61 *Jesus was aware.* (2:24–25.)

62 *What if you should see the Son of Man ascend ... ?* (3:13–15; 5:27; 6:27, 53.) After the resurrection and ascension and the outpouring of the Holy Spirit, many would know that it is indeed possible to be sustained by his life. It would be the kingdom of God coming in power (Mk 9:1).

63 *The flesh has nothing to offer.* That is 'the flesh' as understood by the Jews v. 52. 'The flesh' of Jesus v. 53 is the vehicle of the Spirit that gives life.

64 *Jesus knew from the outset.* v. 61.

65 *No one could come to me unless the Father allows him.* This sounds as if the response to Jesus was pre-destined by the Father. But the meaning is probably that as the initiative is always on God's side attracting people to Christ, and the difficulties are all on the human side, even the weakest response can only be in accordance with the Father's will.

66 *After this, many of his disciples left him.* In their reaction to the teaching of Jesus at Capernaum, the people judged themselves as they rejected or accepted him (5:24); judgement is experienced in the present. This was the end of the ministry in Galilee.

Peter's profession of faith (Mt 16:16–19; Mk 8:27-33)

67 *Do you want to go away too?* In Mk the question was direct, 'Who do you say I am?' In Jn the disciples knew from the beginning that Jesus was the Messiah (1:41, 45, 49). Here their allegiance is being tested.

68 *Simon Peter answered ...* In both versions Peter was the spokesman for the Twelve.

*Lord, who shall we go to? ... we believe ... we
know* ... The Jews had just rejected Jesus because
of what he had said. The disciples accepted him
because of their relationship with him; they trusted
in him and knew from their experience that he was
the Holy One of God.

70 *One of you is a devil.* The disciples did not know who
he was speaking of. In Mk, it was Peter who was
called Satan because he protested at Jesus's prophecy
of his own suffering and death. The words of Jesus
stand as a reminder that the real test of discipleship
is at the moment of crisis.

V. THE FEAST OF TABERNACLES

The Feast of Tabernacles was second in importance
to the Passover. It was obligatory for all men to go
to Jerusalem to celebrate it. In origin it was probably
a festival which came at the end of the grape harvest,
but it had become the annual commemoration of
God's providence during the forty years in the
wilderness when Israel lived in tents. The feast lasted
seven days and the people made light shelters
('tabernacles') in the vineyards and camped there.
Each day there was a solemn libation in the Temple
of water brought from the Pool of Siloam in a golden
vessel. On the first day there was a festival of light.
The Court of the Women in the Temple was full of
lights and all the houses in Jerusalem were lit up.
Water and light are important symbols in this
section.

**Jesus goes up to Jerusalem for the feast and teaches
there**

7:1 *The Jews were out to kill him.* 5:18.

3 *His brothers*. (Mk 6:3.) The belief in the perpetual virginity of Mary is both very ancient and very widely held. The brothers of Jesus could have been sons of Joseph by an earlier marriage, or alternatively any near relation or family friend. In eastern countries 'a brother' can mean anybody you are on familiar terms with.

4 *You should let the whole world see*. (1:10; 3:17.) They did not believe that Jesus was the Messiah, but if he had been sent from God he ought to prove it. It was the theme of the Temptation (Mt 4:5–7).

6 *The right time for me has not yet come*. His 'hour' (2:4). The time has not come for him to manifest his glory on the cross. That time is appointed by the Father and can have nothing to do with the brothers.

11 *The Jews were on the look-out for him*. The religious authorities as distinct from the crowds amongst whom he was the centre of discussion.

14 *Jesus went to the Temple and began to teach*. The last time he was there he had defended himself against an accusation of blasphemy (5:19–47). Now, further teaching about his authority and mission leads the people to wonder if he can be the Messiah. When he cleansed the Temple (2:15–16) he was the Lord coming suddenly in judgement (Malachi 3:1–4) upon abuses. Now he comes in judgement in another way as he challenges the people to accept or reject him (3:18–19).

15 *The Jews were astonished*. (Mk 1:22, 27.) There was a freshness about his teaching that he had plainly never learnt from the rabbis.

16 *My teaching . . . comes . . . from the one who sent me*. No rabbi but the Father himself is the source of the teaching. 'Sent' means 'fully representative' (5:23).

17 *If anyone is prepared to do his will.* .... He will 'be taught by God' (6:45) and know that Jesus is from God.

18 *When he is working for the honour of one who sent him.* (5:23.)

19 *Did not Moses give you the Law?* Jesus had told the Jews before (5:45–47) that Moses and the Law were witnesses on his behalf against them.
Not one of you keeps the Law. For detail about that see Mk 7:1–23.

20 *You are mad!* See 8:48; Mk 3:22; Lk 7:33; Mt 11:18.

21 *One work I did.* The healing of the man at the Pool of Bethzatha (5:1–9).

23 *Circumcision.* A child had to be circumcised on the eighth day after birth. If it were born on the sabbath, it would be due for circumcision on the sabbath. Circumcision was accounted as healing or perfecting; if the healing of one member therefore was allowed on the sabbath, how much more the making 'whole and complete' the man by the pool (5:8, 14).

The people discuss the origin of the Messiah

27 *We all know where he comes from* (1:41, 45; 6:42; Mk 6:3.)

30 *They would have arrested him.* Everything was in the hands of the Father and he could not be touched because the appointed time, his 'hour' had not yet come.

Jesus foretells his approaching departure

31 *When the Christ comes, will he give more signs ... ?* (2:23.) They failed to understand what the signs indicated.

32 *The Pharisees sent Temple police to arrest him.* This
was official action; the proposed arrest of v. 30 was
probably unofficial. The Temple police were controlled by the Chief Priest; the statement that the
Pharisees sent them to effect the arrest shows that
John was out of touch with Jerusalem.

33 *Jesus said.* He was speaking to the people generally,
not only to the police.
I shall go back to the one who sent me. His death
would mean his return to the Father.
You will look for me ... The time would come, at
the final judgement perhaps, when they would seek
his help and it would be too late.
Where I am ... When the Word was made flesh, he
was not separated from the Father (1:38).

35 *The people who are dispersed among the Greeks.* Jews
living in the great cities of the Roman Empire far
outnumbered those in Palestine and were known as
the Dispersion. By the time the gospel was written
Jesus could almost be said to have gone abroad to
teach the Greeks; the Church was by that time
predominantly gentile, or Greek as they were often
called.

The promise of living water

37 *On the last and greatest day of the festival.* Every day
there had been a libation of water in the Temple as a
reminder of God's providence in the wilderness
(Exodus 17:1–7). Christ is God's ultimate gift to his
people.
If any man is thirsty, let him come to me! (4:7, 14;
Isaiah 12:2–3.)

38 *As scripture says* ... The quotation has not been
identified. Notice how the teaching of 6:53 is
repeated here, though in different terms. The 'true'

149

life of the believer is derived from and sustained by Jesus (3:5).

39 *There was no Spirit as yet.* There was never a time when the Spirit did not exist. John was speaking from the point of view of the believers suddenly Spirit-filled at Pentecost (Acts 2:1–13) and made the Church.

Jesus had not yet been glorified. (1:14; 2:11.) The death, resurrection, and ascension of Jesus had to precede the outpouring of the Holy Spirit.

Fresh discussions on the origin of the Messiah

40 *Surely he must be the prophet.* (1:21; 6:14.)

41 *Would the Christ be from Galilee?* Galilee was despised by the people of Judaea. Many gentiles lived there and the inhabitants were not learned in the scriptures and the Law (v. 49).

42 *Does not scripture say ... ?* The passage shows that John knew the Christian tradition about the birth-place of Jesus (Mt 2:4–5; Lk 2:4–7). The Old Testament texts referred to are Micah 5:2 quoted at Mt 2:6 and Psalms 89:3; 132:11.

43 *The people could not agree about him.* Again Jesus brings division as people accept or reject him (5:24; 6:66). See also Lk 12:51–53.

46 *There has never been anybody who has spoken like him.* The police were not prevented by too much learning from responding to the unique authority of Jesus.

49 *This rabble.* (v. 41.) They were simple country people who had come to Jerusalem for the feast.

50 *Nicodemus.* (3:1–21.)

52 *Prophets do not come out of Galilee.* That might be

so but Jesus did not come out of Galilee. He came
from the Father.

The adulterous woman

It is generally agreed that this story (7:53–8:11) was
not written by John. It is omitted in the oldest
versions of the gospel and its vocabulary, style, and
content, are more like Lk than Jn (see Lk 7:37–50).

8:5 *Moses has ordered us in the Law* ... The Law enjoined that both the man and the woman should
be put to death for adultery (Leviticus 20:10). In
this case the man seems to have been allowed to get
away.
What have you to say? It was a trap resembling the
question about tribute to Caesar (Mk 12:13–17). If
he agreed on the death sentence, he could be accused
of usurping the authority of the Roman Governor;
if he did not, he would be disregarding the Law of
Moses.

6 *Jesus started writing on the ground.* What he wrote
can only be guess-work. At the end of a criminal
case, a Roman judge would first write down the
sentence and then read it to the court. It has been
suggested that Jesus, aware of the trap, played the
part of a Roman judge.

7 *If there is one of you who has not sinned* ... The
story is told to drive home the command of Jesus in
the Sermon on the Mount (Mt 7:1–5), 'Do not
judge'. The adultery is not excused, and neither is
the self-righteousness and malice of the accusers.

11 *Don't sin any more.* (5:14.) Jesus had not come to
condemn the world, but to save it (3:17).

Jesus the light of the world

12 *I am the light of the world.* The thought was intro-

duced in the Prologue (1:4–5, 9), and is now illustrated by the illuminations customary at the Feast
of Tabernacles (see the note preceding ch. 7). Jesus
shows people and situations as they really are so that
his disciples can walk 'in the truth'. The language is
derived from the Old Testament (Psalm 27:1;
119:105). We have here another example of the
majestic 'I am' (4:26; 6:35).
Walking in the dark. 'To walk' in both Old and New
Testaments describes the way in which a man faces
life. It will be remembered that 'darkness' symbolises
evil in all its forms (3:19–21).

A discussion on the testimony of Jesus to himself

13 *You are testifying on your own behalf.* (5:31–47.)

14 *Where I came from . . . where I am going.* (7:33.)
You judge by human standards. They could not rid
themselves of the conviction that they knew all about
his origin (6:42; 7:27, 52).
I judge no one. I.e. I condemn no one (3:17–18; 8:11).

16 *But if I judge . . .* The Father has appointed him
supreme judge (5:22, 27; Mt 25; 31–32), and since
he is 'I am' there can be no disputing his decisions.

17 *In your law it is written.* (Deuteronomy 19:15; Jn
5:36–37.) Jesus speaks of 'your' law as being outside
its scope. He was sent by the Father who gave the
Law, is above it, and has come to fulfil it.

20 *No one arrested him.* (7:30.)

The unbelieving Jews warned

21 *I am going away.* (7:33.) The words will recur, and
always refer to the death and resurrection of Jesus,
and his return to the Father.
You will die in your sin. 'Whoever refuses to believe

is condemned already' (3:18). It is the sin against the Holy Spirit (Mt 12:31), preventing them from coming where he is (7:34).

22 *Will he kill himself?* (7:35.) They stumble near the truth but are yet far from it. He laid down his life in order to take it up again (10:17).

23 *You are from below.* They are of this world (1:10; Introduction B. (5)).

24 *I am he.* (4:26; 6:35; 8:12.) Jesus stands in relation to the New Israel, the Church, precisely as Yahweh did to the Old Israel (1:51).

26 *The one who sent me.* Again emphasis on the fact that Jesus was 'sent' (5:23), fully to represent the Father. *What I have learnt . . . I declare to the whole world.* Christ manifests what God is and does, for the whole world to see (1:9, 29; 3:16; 4:42).

28 *When you have lifted up the Son of Man.* (3:14.) The lifting up on the cross is the supreme revelation of the Father's love for the world (3:16), and of the Son's obedience to the Father (4:34). The 'lifting up' is also his exaltation to heaven so that all men may be healed by his saving power (3:5–6, 14; 4:14; 6:51–56).
Then you will know . . . After the resurrection (7:35). *What the Father has taught me.* We are told that Jesus was 'sent' by the Father (5:23), that he 'learnt' from him (8:26), and now that he has been 'taught'. The language is called 'subordinationist' because it suggests that Jesus was subordinate to the Father. In his manhood Jesus was less than the Father, but he was at the same time the pre-existent Word (1:1) as we are reminded by the 'I am' sayings. Acceptance is demanded of us but not comprehension because the subject is beyond the limits of human under-standing.

153

Jesus and Abraham

31 *If you make my word your home.* His 'word' is everything he has taught about himself and his mission,
both through the signs and directly. He is the source
of life and grace (4:14); he is the 'true bread' (6:32);
he is 'the light of the world' (8:12). The disciple
must live with these ideas so that they become part
of him (6:56).

32 *The truth will make you free.* The freedom is from sin
(v. 34). In the light of Christ, evil is shown up for
what it is (8:12). By his grace and strength (4:14;
6:35) it can be overcome.

33 *We are descended from Abraham.* As usual in this
gospel, the Jews take the words of Jesus in their most
literal sense. Many seem to have believed that
salvation was theirs by right of descent from Abraham
(Mt 3:9).
We have never been slaves of anyone. This was not
true. There had been the captivity in Egypt from
which Moses had freed them and when the kingdom
of David crumbled, they had been subjected by one
great empire after another. Rome was just the last
of a series. Through it all however, they had retained
their distinctive beliefs and way of life.

35 *The slave's place . . . the son's place.* Different types
of relationship are represented by 'the slave', and
'the son'. The true kinsman of Jesus is 'anyone who
does the will of God' (Mk 3:35) regardless of
descent. Conversely, anyone who does not do the
will of God is like a slave, Jew though he may be.

39 *If you were Abraham's children you would do as
Abraham did.* Faith was Abraham's outstanding
virtue. He trusted God, confident that he would keep
his promise (Genesis 12:1–3) although it seemed
impossible of fulfilment. The Jews were certainly of

Abraham's race, but without his faith and obedience they were not his true children. St Paul reasoned on similar lines (Galatians 4:21–31).

41 *We were not born of prostitution.* They meant that they were descendants of Abraham by his wife Sara, not by Hagar the slave from whom were descended the despised Ishmaelites. Also they were not tainted with idolatry (4:16) and had always kept the Law. There is a possible reference here as well to what was reported about the birth of Jesus in anti-Christian circles.

43 *You are unable to understand my language.* 'To those who are outside everything comes in parables' (Mk 4:11–12; Isaiah 6:9–10).

44 *A murderer from the start.* The allusion is to the story of Adam and Eve in the garden of Eden (Genesis 3). Eve listened to the serpent's lie and then disobeyed God. As a result, death came into the world.

48 *A Samaritan and possessed by the devil.* See the introduction to ch. 4. The Samaritans were believed by the Jews to be descended from the illegitimate offspring of Israelite women and foreign colonists. The innuendo of v. 41 is being repeated. For the accusation that he was mad see Mk 3:22–30.

49 *I honour my Father.* (5:23.)

51 *Whoever keeps my word.* (v. 31.)
Will never see death. There are two kinds of life, one born of the flesh and the other of the Spirit (3:5–6; 5:24). The life born of the Spirit is not destroyed by physical death (6:57–58).

52 *Know the taste of death.* Those were not the words of Jesus. They had failed to understand his language (v. 43).

54 *If I were to seek my own glory* ... What people generally consider glory, is not glory at all. The glory of Jesus will be seen when he 'is lifted up' (3:14–15; 8:28).

55 *I faithfully keep his word.* (v. 28.)

56 *Abraham rejoiced to think that he would see my Day.* The rabbis taught that when Abraham was old, he was shown 'the age to come' and the days of the Messiah.

57 *You are not fifty yet.* The only other reference to the age of Jesus during his ministry is at Lk 3:23. 'When he started to teach, Jesus was about thirty years old'.

58 *Before Abraham ever was, I AM.* (1:1; 4:26; 5:17–18; 6:35; 7:37; 8:12.)
It has been remarked that if Jesus was not what he claimed to be, he was not even a good man.

59 *They took up stones.* Stoning was the penalty for blasphemy (5:18). But his 'hour' had not yet come and he slipped away unharmed (Lk 4:30).

The cure of the man born blind (5th sign)

9:2 *Who sinned, this man or his parents ... ?* The common explanation for suffering was that it was a punishment for sin. The gospels are consistent in showing that Jesus said it was not so (Lk 13:2–4).

3 *That the works of God might be displayed in him.* It sometimes seems impossible to reconcile the idea of the goodness of God with the anguish of innocent people. But such suffering, bravely and patiently borne, can be an inspiration to those who see it, and a creative force in them. It is the idea behind the Suffering Servant Songs (1:29; particularly Isaiah 52:13–53:12). Self-pity on the other hand is a destroying force.

4 *As long as the day lasts.* 'The day' is the earthly life of Jesus.
The night will soon be here. His death.

6 *He spat on the ground, made a paste with the spittle* . . .
Jesus was using a common first-century medical technique; spittle was believed to have healing properties (Mk 7:33; 8:23). But more than physical healing is implied here. In Genesis 2:6-7, after the earth had been watered, 'Yahweh God fashioned man of dust from the soil'. We are to understand that the blind man had been totally re-fashioned by Jesus, the Word and Creator (1:3).

7 *Go and wash in the Pool of Siloam.* The Feast of Tabernacles was not yet ended and it was from this pool that water was taken for the libation in the Temple (7:37), water which represented all God's merciful provision for his people (4:7). It is carefully explained here that the name Siloam means 'sent', and throughout the gospel stress is laid on the fact that Jesus was 'sent' by the Father (4:34; 5:36; 6:29 etc.). Going to wash in the pool, therefore, was to find cleansing in Jesus and insight to believe and to worship him (v. 38). The man was like those of the post-resurrection Church, 'born through water and the Spirit' (3:5).

9 *I am the man.* He was changed beyond recognition. The washing and gift of sight made evident the person he was meant to be, a true kinsman of Jesus (8:35).

14 *It had been a sabbath.* It was the familiar subject of controversy (5:10). 'The Law was given through Moses, grace and truth have come through Jesus Christ' (1:17).

16 *Some of the Pharisees said* . . . *Others said.* Jesus

157

was again the centre of controversy and division (6:66; 7:12, 43). See also Lk 12:51-52.

17 *He is a prophet.* (4:19.)

22 *The Jews ... agreed to expel from the synagogue ...* This is the perspective of the early Church. During the ministry of Jesus, the people were puzzled as to the identity of Jesus and only the Twelve recognised him as Messiah (Mk 8:27-38), and then they did not understand at all what he told them about his mission. The threat of formal expulsion from the synagogue on the issue could not have arisen.

24 *Give glory to God!* This was the formula for putting someone on oath to tell the truth.

29 *As for this man, we don't know where he comes from.* They sometimes thought they knew (6:42; 7:41), but Jesus had warned them not to be too sure (7:14).

31 *God does listen to men who are devout.* The man reasoned like Nicodemus (3:2).

34 *They drove him away.* He was expelled from the synagogue.

35 *The Son of Man.* For the implications of this title see particularly 5:27; 6:53, 62. Other references, 1:51; 3:13; 6:27; 8:28.

37 *You are looking at him; he is speaking to you.* It was the moment of crisis, the test of the newly received gift of vision. For the theme of seeing and believing see 1:19-51 and the introductory note.

38 *The man said, 'Lord, I believe', and worshipped him.* This is the Christian affirmation of faith (1 Corinthians 12:3). The man worships, not in the Temple but at the feet of Jesus (2:19-22), and in so doing worships the Father 'in spirit and in truth' (4:23).

The sign demonstrates the supersession of Moses and the Law by Jesus (1:17).

39 *It is for judgement that I have come.* (3:17–18; 5:22.) Jesus is the light of the world (8:12). He bestows vision, and in his light the real and the false show up for what they are.

41 *Since you say, "We see", your guilt remains.* The Pharisees were the 'blind guides' of Mt 23:16.

The good shepherd

The general application of this passage cannot be missed. In its context in the gospel however, it is a comment on the healing of the blind man, the Good Shepherd being contrasted with the bad shepherds who had driven him away (9:34). The symbolism is derived from the Old Testament, Ezekiel 34:11–31 being particularly relevant. Jesus went to find the man healed by the Pool of Bethzatha (5:14), and then the blind man (9:35); his searches recall the synoptic parable of the lost sheep (Mt 18:12–14// Lk 15:6–7). There is a certain fluidity in the figures used here and it is a mistake to attempt detailed interpretation of them.

10:1 *The sheepfold.* The picture reflects what is still the common practice in some parts of the Middle East. The flocks are taken into the courtyards at sunset, and out again in the early morning. The sheepfold represents Israel, called by God at Sinai to be a consecrated nation (Exodus 19:6) and now being called by Christ to be the New Israel (1:47–51).
A thief and brigand. These probably typify the religious authorities who broke the fundamental law of God, which demands justice, mercy and humility (Mk 7:1–13), and robbed the people of their freedom as sons of God (8:35) by burdening them with regulations which no one could keep.

2 *The one who enters through the gate.* Only the shepherd has the right of entry to the fold, and the right to tend the flock. Jesus is the true Messiah, anointed by the Holy Spirit (1:33), descended from David (7:42), sent by the Father.

3 *One by one he calls his own sheep.* In some versions of the gospel he calls each 'by his own name'. A vitally important characteristic of the Good News is its insistence on the unique value of every single individual (6:39-40; Lk 15:4).
   He ... leads them out. The first members of the Church were Jews, led out from the Old Israel to form the New Israel.

4 *He goes ahead of them.* Shepherds in eastern countries always go ahead of their flocks. The Church goes wrong when it fails to listen to Christ and follow him. For an example of the Holy Spirit directing the Church see Acts 13:3-4.

6 *Jesus told them this parable but they failed to understand.* I.e. the Pharisees (9:40).

7 *I am the gate of the sheepfold.* This is another of the 'I am' sayings (4:26; 6:35; 8:12, 58). It is only through Jesus that the members of the flock can find security, in the New Israel which is his Church. Equally, only those authorised by Jesus can enter to deputise for him as shepherds, v. 1 (20:21; 21:15).

8 *All others who have come ...* The immediate reference is probably to the Pharisees (9:40; Mt 23:1-36), but in the prophetic books of the Old Testament there are many allusions to leaders of the people who in their day, played much the same part.
   The sheep took no notice of them. There were always faithful ones capable of recognising what was false.

9 *He will go freely in and out.* (8:32.) Totally com-

mitted in his obedience to the Father, he is not in bondage to sin. Completely trusting the Father he does not fear what people or circumstances can do to him.

Sure of finding pasture. (4:14; 6:48.)

10 *I have come so that they may have life.* This was the whole purpose of his mission. The life he came to give is 'eternal life' (3:15–16), described in the Prologue as 'fullness' (1:16–17) and pictured in the story of the miracle at Cana.

11 *I am the good shepherd,* 4:26; 6:35; 8:12, 58; 10:7. *The good shepherd . . . lays down his life for the sheep.* This is a reference to the crucifixion, but everyone knew that shepherding was dangerous work. Flocks had sometimes to be defended from the attacks of wild animals.

12 *The hired man.* He cares only for his wages and his safety. He differs from the thief and brigand who want to take over the control of the flock.
The wolf attacks and scatters the sheep. The wolf is the figure in the New Testament for teachers who try to turn people from the truth (Mt 7:15; Acts 20:29).

14 *I know my own.* This is the knowledge of personal relationship. In v. 3 the shepherd calls each of his sheep, one by one. The relationship between the Father and the Son is reflected in the relationship between the Son and the disciple.

16 *There are other sheep I have.* These are not called forth from the original fold, Israel (v. 1), but from among the gentiles or Greeks as they were often called (7:35).
There will be only one flock. The New Israel will be composed of many different peoples united in their allegiance to Christ. There were breakaway groups

(schisms) in the Church almost from the beginning of its history. These developed into the distinctive Churches we have today: Roman Catholic, Church of England, Protestant Churches of different kinds, etc. A movement towards unity began early in this century and has been growing steadily. It is becoming ever more widely understood that it is a scandal for Christians to be separated, and that Christ means them to be 'one flock'.

17–18 *I lay down my life . . . of my own free will.* This is a point on which John places particular emphasis. The initiative was always with Jesus (Mt 26:53). He laid down his life that the power of the resurrection might draw all men to him for healing and life (3:14–15).

19 *These words caused disagreement among the Jews.* (6:66; 7:12, 40–44; 9:16.)

VI. THE FEAST OF DEDICATION

Jesus claims to be the Son of God

22 *The Feast of Dedication.* Antiochus Epiphanes, gentile king of a region which included Syria and Palestine, defiled the Temple in 167 B.C. by placing a statue of Zeus there, and causing sacrifice to be offered to it. Three years later, the Temple was captured by Jewish patriots, purified and re-dedicated. The Feast of Dedication was the annual celebration of this event.

It was winter. The feast was celebrated in December, about two months after the Feast of Tabernacles.

23 *The Portico of Solomon.* This was an arcade sheltered from the cold, a favourite place of teachers.

24 *If you are the Christ, tell us plainly.* (Lk 22:67.) The question recalls the trial of Jesus before the Sanhedrin, the Great Council.

25 *I have told you.* He had only told the Samaritan woman in plain terms (4:26), but he had made it quite clear to the Jews that he spoke as God's envoy (5:17f; 6:32f; 8:28–29, 56–58).
The works I do in my Father's name are my witness. (5:36.)

30 *The Father and I are one.* (5:17.) God is uniquely to be seen in Jesus. What Jesus does and says is what God does and says.

31 *The Jews fetched stones . . .* (5:18; 8:59.)

34 *Your Law.* (8:17.)
I said, you are gods. (Psalm 82:6.) Jesus was arguing from scripture like a rabbi. The words of the psalm were as if addressed to magistrates who acted as God's representatives in their work (Deuteronomy 1:17). Jesus represented the Father as his opponents could not.

35 *Scripture cannot be rejected.* Scripture was understood literally as the word of God. Its language was sacrosanct.

36 *Someone the Father has consecrated.* At the feast of Dedication the consecration of the Temple was naturally the subject uppermost in men's minds. Jesus was consecrated (1:33) to show the love of the Father for the world (3:16–17). He was to be the new Temple where alone men could worship 'in spirit and truth' (2:19; 4:24; 9:38).

39 *They wanted to arrest him.* (7:30, 44; 8:38.)

Jesus withdraws to the other side of Jordan (Mk 10:1)
40 *He went back again to the far side of Jordan.* Jesus

had been rejected in Galilee and in Jerusalem his life was threatened. He now returned briefly to the place of his 'consecration' (1:33) before going up to Jerusalem for his Passion, the climax of his mission (12:32).

The resurrection of Lazarus (6th sign)

Viewed simply as an event within the gospel story as a whole, this miracle is important because it precipitated the arrest of Jesus. It was a crisis point. The deliberate contrast between the raising of Lazarus who stumbled from the tomb bound hand and foot, and the resurrection of Jesus whose grave clothes were left like a shell (20:3–10) is intended to underline the difference between common humanity and Jesus, the Word made flesh. But before all else the miracle was a sign, pointing to the fact that Jesus is the Lord and Giver of life, and it is particularly from that point of view that it must be studied. It has been made clear that life is of two kinds, of the flesh and of the spirit (3:5). We know that death certainly comes to the one and the gospel implies that it can come to the other (3:16). But flesh and spirit are alike under the dominion of Christ, and those who keep his word 'will never see death' (8:51). Behind the story lies the experience of the Christian community of the power of the Risen Christ using ordinary people to effect his healing purposes. Of less relevance to modern Christians is the possible identification of Lazarus with the Old Israel. The community within which the story was first told was probably close to its Jewish origins; Israel was envisaged as being done to death by the massive regulations of the Law of Moses (Romans 7:7–25), and raised to life and freedom by Christ's gift of grace (1:16; 8:32).

11:1 *Bethany*. The village was on the Mount of Olives, just outside Jerusalem.
Two sisters, Martha and Mary. Mentioned in Lk (Lk 10:38–42) and not elsewhere. For the story of the anointing see 12:1–11.

3 *The sisters sent ... to Jesus*. If it is correct that the story reflects the experience of the community, the sisters can be understood as intercessors, the Church being a family of believers. It will be noticed that they asked nothing definite of Jesus. The trouble was simply laid before him.

4 *This sickness will not end in death but in God's glory*. The glory of God (his saving activity) was manifested in Christ's work of power in raising Lazarus from the dead. The death of Jesus which was the direct result (11:47–53) was the supreme manifestation of God's glory.

6 *He stayed where he was for two more days*. The supernatural knowledge of Jesus is emphasised in this gospel (2:25; 6:70) and he knew that Lazarus was already dead, vv. 11, 13, 17. He knew also that when he went to Jerusalem it would be to his death, his 'hour' determined by the Father. He would go when the right time came.

7 *Let us go to Judaea*. 'His own country' (4:44).

9 *Are there not twelve hours in the day?* The ministry of Jesus was short and he had to make full use of the time available.
The light of this world. The comparison of course is with Jesus, the 'true light that enlightens all men' (1:9; 8:12).

11 *Lazarus is resting*. The first Christians, in sure hope of the resurrection, commonly described death as 'falling asleep'.

15 *I am glad I was not there.* Trust in Jesus cannot be known for what it is unless it is tested.

16 *Thomas . . . said . . . 'Let us go too, and die with him'.* In the synoptic gospels Thomas is only mentioned in the lists of the Twelve (Mt 10:3; Mk 3:18; Lk 6:15). 'To die with Christ' was St Paul's expression for true discipleship. It derives from a saying of Jesus (Mk 8:34; Romans 6:6).

17 *In the tomb for four days.* Humanly speaking the situation was irreversible.

20 *Martha . . . went to meet him. Mary remained . . .* As in Lk 10:38–42 Martha is the active one while Mary sits quietly. They may be intended to represent the two main types of discipleship, the active and the contemplative.

21 *If you had been here, my brother would not have died.* 'Anyone who has the Son has life, anyone who does not have the Son does not have life' (I John 5:12). Again, as in v. 3, nothing definite was asked for. The matter was left in the hands of Jesus.

24 *The resurrection on the last day.* (5:25.) The Pharisees believed in the resurrection of the dead; the Sadducees did not (Mk 12:18–27).

25 *I am the resurrection.* Many versions add 'and the life'. This is one of the most important of the 'I am' sayings (4:26; 6:35; 8:12, 58; 10:7, 11). The resurrection is to be understood not only as a future event (5:24–29) but a present Christian experience which results from trust in and obedience to Jesus.
Even though he dies he will live. Physical death is only incidental. The life born of the Spirit (3:5–6) is continuous because Jesus sustains with his own life those who believe in him (1:12; 4:14; 6:56–58; 8:51).

27 *I believe that you are the Christ* ... This statement of belief is like an early Christian creed, one of several of which there are traces in the New Testament. They were formulated to ensure that people seeking baptism were clear about what they were expected to believe.

28 *The Master is here.* The English words are very ordinary but in Greek they call to mind the expectation of Christ's coming at the end of time, the Parousia (Mk 13:26). 'His own' are on the watch for his coming (Mk 13:35-37), and where two meet in his name, he will be with them (Mt 18:19). Martha spoke low because the Jewish visitors could not share in the hope of disciples.

31 *Going to the tomb to weep.* The ritual weeping common in the east.

32 *Mary went to Jesus.* Mary's action and words were the same as Martha's. Repetition was a literary technique to achieve emphasis. The Church which acknowledges Jesus as 'the Christ, the Son of God' (v. 27) must wait for his will to be made clear.

33 *Jesus* ... *in great distress.* Our version suggests simply that he shared in the suffering of the bereaved sisters and shed tears of sympathy. But the Greek word used implies sternness as at Mk 1:45. It is possible that we are to understand that he knew that the forthcoming miracle would be the excuse for his arrest, and his foreknowledge weighed heavily upon him.

38 *It was a cave with a stone to close the opening.* It was a rock tomb of the kind in which the body of Jesus would so soon be laid. The whole emphasis is on the finality of death.

39 *Take the stone away.* The sisters had earlier brought

their brother's plight to the attention of Jesus. Now again, ordinary people have their part to play in co-operating with Christ in bringing life out of death. If the story is intended to show the power of Christ to re-create a man totally given to sin, the stone represents whatever obstacle blocks his response to Christ; respect for convention perhaps, ignorance, or habit. If we are to see in Lazarus the Old Israel, the obstacle is the 'preaching a crucified Christ' (I Corinthians 1:23); Jews argued that God would never have allowed his 'Anointed One' to suffer a criminal's death.

41 *Father, I thank you for hearing my prayer* ... The communion between the Father and the Son is perfect and unbroken (8:29). Sent by the Father, Jesus has the authority to quicken the dead (5:19–30). *I speak for the sake of all these* ... The communion of the Father and the Son is to be reflected in the believing disciples so that they may be one in the Father and the Son (17:21).

44 *The dead man came out.* The life of the flesh and the life of the spirit are equally the gift of the Son. Lazarus, like the prodigal son, had been dead and was alive again (Lk 15:32).

44 *Unbind him, let him go free.* Again there was something for ordinary people to do (vv. 3, 39). The Church is Christ's body, his agent in the world. He gave the apostles the authority to bind and to loose, to forgive sins on his behalf (Mt 16:19; 18:39; Jn 20:22–23). A person crippled by a sense of guilt can sometimes only be freed by receiving absolution from a priest. At their ordination all priests are empowered to do this. Lazarus was restored to newness of life of either kind, of the flesh or the spirit, and that life was 'in' Jesus (1:4).

The Jewish leaders decide on the death of Jesus

45 *Many of the Jews ... believed ... but some ... As* on other occasions Jesus caused division; the process of judgement came into operation (3:18–19; 5:24; 6:66; 7:12, 31, 41).

47 *The chief priests and the Pharisees called a meeting.* It would have been a meeting of the Sanhedrin, the Great council responsible for Jewish affairs.

48 *If we let him go on in this way ...* By taking action against Jesus they brought about the results they wanted to avoid. Christians were accused of having turned the world upside down by the time the gospel was written (Acts 17:6).
The Romans will come and destroy the Holy Place and our nation. The Jewish war against the Romans ended in 70 with the destruction of Jerusalem and the Temple, and the extinction of the Jewish nation until its resurgence in modern times.

49 *Caiaphas, the high priest that year.* (Mt 26:3; Lk 3:2.) Caiaphas was continuously in office from A.D. 18 until 36.

50 *It is better for one man to die for the people.* He argued that the Romans would take punitive action if Jesus was generally acclaimed as Messiah.

52 *Not for the nation only.* The death of Jesus was necessary for the salvation of the whole world. The universality of his mission is stressed throughout the gospel (3:16-17; 4:42; 7:35; 10:16).
The scattered children of God. (1:12; 10:16.)

53 *From that day they were determined to kill him.* The raising of Lazarus was the reason for the plot to kill him.

54 *A town called Ephraim.* This was in Judaea, not far from Jerusalem.

VII. THE LAST PASSOVER

A. BEFORE THE PASSION

The Passover draws near

55 *The Jewish Passover drew near.* (2:13; 6:4.) This is
the last of the three recorded in the gospel. The
consistent emphasis on the fact that it was Jewish is
an important reminder of its supersession so soon
to be effected.

*Many . . . had gone up to Jerusalem to purify them-
selves.* The Jewish rites of purification were inadequate as the story of the marriage feast at Cana
was intended to show (2:6).

56 *Will he come to the festival or not?* Jesus, the 'lamb
of God that takes away the sin of the world' was
going up to Jerusalem to his death which would be
the one, true, and effective means of overcoming sin
(1:29).

The anointing at Bethany (Mt 26:6–13; Mk 14:3–9)

The story of the anointing at Bethany is in all the
gospels except Lk, and only in Jn is the woman
named. In Lk there is another story of Jesus being
anointed earlier in his ministry by a woman who was
a sinner (Lk 7:36–50), identified for centuries with
Mary, an identification now known to be late and
therefore not generally accepted. In Mt//Mk the
ointment was poured upon the head of Jesus,
suggesting that the act was a recognition of his kingship though he received it as anticipating the anointing of his body after death. In Lk and Jn the feet of
Jesus were anointed and wiped with the woman's
hair, a gesture of penitence in the first case as well as
devotion in both. The different versions of the story

are complementary. The kingship of Jesus (his universal rule) is inseparably connected with his death (13:14–15; 12:32), and his saving power, demonstrated by his forgiveness of sins in Luke's story, becomes universally operative after his death and resurrection.

12:1 *Jesus went to Bethany where Lazarus was.* Lazarus is specifically mentioned as a reminder that Jesus is the resurrection (11:25), a hint that the story which follows has a bearing on the Passion.

2 *They gave a dinner for him there.* Mark says that the dinner was in the house of Simon the leper. John does not imply more than that Lazarus was a guest. The repetition of his name underlines the hint.

3 *Mary ... anointed the feet of Jesus.* It was the customary mark of respect for an honoured guest, but Mary's generosity and humility are presented here as an example of true discipleship which reflects Christ's self-offering on the cross.
The house was full of the scent of the ointment. Behind the factual statement there probably lies interpretation of the saying of Jesus, 'Wherever throughout all the world the Good News is proclaimed, what she has done will be told also, in remembrance of her' (Mk 14:9). The Church was often described as the household of God in early times.

4 *Judas Iscariot.* He is not mentioned in the other versions of the story.

5 *Three hundred denarii.* A denarius was the average daily wage of a manual worker. The ointment was very expensive indeed.

6 *He was a thief.* (Jn only.) He 'had charge of the common fund' (13:29). The information that he

171

sold Jesus to the authorities is in Mt only (Mt 26:14–16).

10 *The chief priests decided to kill Lazarus as well.* (11:47–48.)

The Messiah enters Jerusalem (Mt 21:1–11; Mk 11:1–10; Lk 19:29–40)

13 *Branches of palm.* (Jn only.) When the Temple was freed from pagan occupation (10:22) before re-dedication, the people waved branches of palm in honour of Simon Maccabaeus, the victor. The detail is a subtle reminder that in the person of Jesus, the Temple will be superseded (1:19–21).
Hosanna! Blessings on the King of Israel ... The words are an adaptation of Psalm 118:26, a Passover Psalm which would come naturally to mind (Mt 21:9; Mk 11:9–10; Lk 19:38). 'Hosanna' means 'Save, now'. The title is used only in this account of the entry, and the story of the anointing has been placed immediately before it instead of afterwards as in Mt//Mk, in order to show Jesus as entering Jerusalem as its anointed king. Jesus had been greeted as King of Israel at the beginning of the gospel by Nathanael (1:49).

14 *Jesus found a young donkey.* Synoptic detail about his preparations is omitted, but it is clear that Jesus intended to convey the truth about himself by what he did, as when he cleansed the Temple (2:15), by a prophetic act as it is called.
As scripture says. Zechariah 9:9; quoted at Mt 21:5.

15 *Daughter of Zion.* A poetic expression for Jerusalem, frequently used by Old Testament writers.
Your king is coming, mounted on the colt of a donkey. Kings rode donkeys when they came in peace.

16 *At the time his disciples did not understand this.* (2:22.)

172

17 *All who had been with him when he called Lazarus ...*
They bore witness to Christ's dominion over death,
foreshadowing the witness of the New Israel to the
resurrection of Jesus himself.

19 *The whole world is running after him.* Judaism could
do nothing to counteract the attractive power of
Christ, King of the New Israel, 'saviour of the world'
(1:49; 4:42; 11:47–48).

Jesus foretells his death and subsequent glorification

20 *Some Greeks.* (Introduction B. (4); 7:35.) They had
come to Jerusalem to keep the feast as far as they
were allowed, and are mentioned here as representative of 'the whole world' (v. 19).

21 *These approached Philip.* (1:40, 43; 6:5, 8.) The
Greek approach to Jesus was through men with
Greek names.

23 *Jesus replied to them.* No more is heard of the Greeks
and the words which follow suggest that the time is
not ripe. They can only come to him after his death
and resurrection.
Now has the hour come ... Note the particular
significance of 'hour' (1:14; 7:30; 8:20), 'Son of
Man' (1:51; 3:13–14; 6:53), 'glory', 'glorified'
(1:14; 7:39).

24 *Unless a grain of wheat falls on the ground and dies ...*
Only by his death and resurrection could the very
life of Christ become available to indwell and
sustain all who believe in him (1:12; 6:51–53; 7:
38–39).

25 *Anyone who loves his life loses it.* (Mk 8:35.) The
disciple must follow Christ in self-giving or he will
lose the 'true' life which is in Christ.
Anyone who hates his life in this world ... The word

translated 'hate' often means 'to put into second place'. God must have absolute priority.

27 *Now my soul is troubled.* The story of the agony in Gethsemane is not included in Jn but vv. 27–28 are reminiscent of it (Mk 14:34–36).
What shall I say? In Gethsemane he prayed, 'Let it be as you, not I would have it' (Mk 14:36). Already great stress has been laid on the identity of will as between the Father and the Son (5:30).
It was for this very reason. If the grain dies 'it yields a rich harvest' (v. 23).

28 *Father, glorify your name.* God is glorified by the complete obedience of his Son who desires only the glory of the Father. 'Name' is indicative of personality and God's love for the world is supremely manifested in the death and resurrection of Jesus.
A voice came from heaven. A rabbinic way of saying 'God spoke' (Mk 1:11; 9:7).

29 *It was an angel speaking to him.* (Lk 22:43.)

30 *It was not for my sake that this voice came.* The bystanders had heard a sound but had been unable to interpret it. They were probably aware nevertheless that what Jesus had said about his death and glorification was confirmed by God.

31 *Now sentence is being passed on this world.* (3:18–19.) In their reaction to Jesus men pass sentence on themselves (9:35–41).
The prince of this world. Satan had the whole world in his grip (Mk 3:27).

32 *When I am lifted up from the earth ...* The lifting up on the cross will precede his resurrection and return to the Father (7:33–34). All men will then see Jesus (vv. 20–22), and seeing, will believe and worship him (9:38; 11:25).

34 *The Law has taught us* . . . The scriptures as a whole.
Who is this Son of Man? (v. 23.)

35 *The light will be with you only a little longer.* (11:9–11.)
Walk while you have the light. Believe before it is too
late.

36 *Jesus left them.* This was the end of his public
ministry.

Conclusion: the unbelief of the Jews

37 *They did not believe in him.* Devout Jews who became
Christian, notably St Paul, were deeply concerned to
see why it was, after God had given such rich
privileges to his people, that the Messiah was rejected
when at last he came (Romans 9:1–5).

38 *This was to fulfil the words of the prophet Isaiah.*
(Isaiah 6:9f.) They saw the rejection as being some-
how within the mysterious purpose of God and
foretold by the prophets.

41 *Isaiah said this when he saw his glory.* 'I saw the Lord
Yahweh seated on a high throne' (Isaiah 6:1). If any
doubts remain as to John's conviction about the
divinity of Jesus, this text should dispel them.

42 *Yet there were many who did believe in him.* Nicodemus was one (3:1; 7:50–52; 19:39), and Joseph
of Arimathaea (19:38).
Fear of being expelled from the synagogue. (9:22.)

44 *Jesus declared publicly* . . . The following lines sum
up the teaching given by Jesus to the general public.
Chs. 14–16 contain teaching given privately to his
disciples.

B. THE LAST SUPPER

The account of the supper in this gospel differs

considerably from the synoptics. (i) It was not the passover meal, but took place the evening before. (ii) There is no mention of the institution of the Eucharist. The instruction in ch. 6:22–66 presupposes knowledge of the rite. (iii) In Jn the supper begins with the washing of the disciples' feet, an acted parable not found elsewhere, foreshadowing the death of Jesus and its benefits. Particularly as we come to the closing scenes in our Lord's earthly life, it is important always to remember that John's purpose was not primarily to teach facts—his readers were sufficiently familiar with them (1:29, 45; 6:42)—but to explain how and why the death and resurrection of Jesus, and his return to the Father, are dynamic in the everyday lives of believers.

Jesus washes his disciples' feet

13:1 *It was before the festival of the Passover.* John may well have had good historical grounds for making this statement, but its importance for him was theological. (Introduction D.) Jesus was dying on the cross when the lambs were being ritually slain in the Temple in preparation for the feast which began at sunset. Jesus is thus seen as the Lamb of God (1:29), the true Passover (I Corinthians 5:7).
Jesus knew that the hour had come. (2:4; 7:30; 8:8; 12:23.)
He had always loved those that were his. The love of Jesus has been implied by his actions but is only explicitly mentioned in connection with the family at Bethany (11:3, 5). It becomes a major theme and it is important to be alert to its definition.

2 *They were at supper.* John does not, as has already been pointed out, record the institution of the Eucharist. Its sacrificial aspect which derives from the synoptic accounts (Mt 26:26–28; Mk 14:22–24;

Lk 22:19-20) has been dealt with at 6:48-59, and he has preferred to present it in terms of the Messianic banquet which would inaugurate the kingdom of God (2:1; 6:11). Thought of the costliness of Christ's self-offering nevertheless is intrinsic to the entire passage.

The devil had already put it into the mind of Judas. All the evangelists saw the ministry and Passion of Jesus as a conflict with Satan and all the powers of darkness (Mk 3:27; Lk 10:17-18). The sinister element is emphasised by further reference at vv. 11, 18 before the announcement at v. 21.

3 *Jesus knew ... that he had come from God ...* The words suggest the immeasurable condescension of the Word made flesh. He humbled himself in becoming man, and he would humble himself to the depths in submitting to a criminal's death (Philippians 2:5-10).

4 *He got up from table.* What he was about to do teaches three things. It is a revelation of the character of God, for Jesus who does it is God. It sets a pattern for his disciples to follow. It demonstrates how his death will be effective in the lives of believers.

(He) ... removed his outer garment. He will die and lay aside the limitations of ordinary humanity.

5 *He began to wash the disciples' feet.* It was customary for a slave to wash the feet of guests on their arrival. Now it was the host himself who did it.

6 *He came to Simon Peter.* Peter's impulsive reaction was characteristic (Mk 8:27-32). He was quite sure he knew best.

7 *At the moment you do not know ... later you will understand.* (2:17; 12:16.)

8 *If I do not wash you, you can have nothing in common*

with me. The spirit equally with the flesh (3:6) needs cleansing. The Holy Spirit, released into the world after the death and resurrection of Jesus, works within us, directing our minds and wills and strengthening us to fight against evil inclinations. This process is described in the ancient language of the Church as being 'cleansed by his most precious Blood'.

10 *No one who has taken a bath needs washing.* Many authorities add 'except for his feet'. Guests would have bathed before setting out for the feast, but their feet would get dirty on the way there. We are probably to understand that the bath is baptism, the moment of decision for Christ made once and for all when the spirit is cleansed and the Holy Spirit given. But the way through life is often difficult and dangerous and frequent washing—the forgiveness of our sins—is necessary before we can have something in common with him (v. 8).

11 *He knew who was going to betray him.* (v. 2.)

14 *You should wash each other's feet.* (See v. 4.) Jesus had performed the humblest service for all his disciples, including his betrayer. His disciples were not to consider their dignity when helping others, and that other kind of cleansing was to be continued among them by their forgiveness of one another and their mutual assurance of the forgiveness of the Father.

16 *No servant is greater than his master.* (Mt 10:24; Lk 22:24–27.)

18 *I know the ones I have chosen.* 'He could tell what a man had in him' (2:25), and he had always known about Judas (6:70–71).
What scripture says must be fulfilled. (Psalm 41:9.) It was all under the control of God. See also 10:34–35.

178

19 *I tell you this now, before it happens* . . . When the
prediction of Jesus is fulfilled, they will know that
in him they see God.

20 *Whoever welcomes the one I send welcomes me.*
(2:21; Mt. 10:40.)

The treachery of Judas foretold (Mt 26:21–25; Mk
14:17–21; Lk 22:21–23)

21 *Jesus was troubled in spirit.* (11:33; 12:27.) He was
God (v. 19) but fully man as well.
Jesus . . . declared . . . one of you will betray me. (v. 2.)
The final phase of the conflict has begun (Mt 26:21–
22; Mk 14:18–19; Lk 22:21).

23 *The disciple Jesus loved.* This is the first mention of
the unnamed disciple identified as John himself in
the earliest tradition (Introduction A.). Everyone
reclined on the left side leaving the right hand free
for use. The disciple was next to Jesus and in such a
position that he could speak to him without being
overheard.

26 *The piece of bread.* This was not the bread of the
Eucharist but it was part of the meal they had all
shared, and treachery against people you have fed
with has always been regarded as the worst kind.
Like Luke, John has placed the prediction of the
betrayal at the end of the supper and not at the
beginning like Mt//Mk.

27 *After Judas had taken the bread, Satan entered him.*
Receiving the bread did not make Judas the instru-
ment of Satan. It was the moment when he allowed
Satan control.

30 *Night had fallen.* Supper would have started soon
after sunset and it was now getting late. John was
not thinking of the time however but that Judas had

179

left the light of Christ to go out into spiritual darkness
(1:4; 3:19).

31 *Now has the Son of Man been glorified.* It was as if
the Passion was already accomplished with the
submission of Judas to Satan. The humility and
obedience of Jesus to the Father fully revealed on
the cross, had been anticipated in the washing of the
feet, and his troubled spirit (v. 21) was a reminder
of the cost of his self-offering. Notice how consistently the title Son of Man is linked with the idea
of the glorification of Jesus (1:51; 3:13–14; 5:27;
8:28; 12:23, 32, 34).

32 *God will in turn glorify him in himself.* 'Himself'
refers to the Father who will glorify the Son by
taking him to himself in glory.
Very soon. After the resurrection Jesus will return
to the Father and his universal rule will begin (Mt
28:18–20).

Farewell discourses

33 *My little children.* The Lord loves 'his own' and
knows how weak they are.
As I told the Jews. (7:34; 8:21.)

34 *I give you a new commandment.* They cannot go
where he is going except by dying. Obedience to the
new commandment will prepare them for that.
Love one another; just as I have loved you. (v. 1.) The
depth and character of his love, already exemplified
(v. 31), will soon be made clearer on the cross. See
the synoptic form of the commandment, cited from
the Old Testament (Mk 12:31; Leviticus 19:18).

35 *By this love . . . everyone will know that you are my
disciples.* It has been said that in the very early years
of the Church, the gentiles at Antioch were so
impressed by the active care of its members for one

another that they nicknamed them the 'kindly ones' (in Greek 'chrestoi'), and our word 'Christian' derives from that. This is, however, an unlikely derivation.

36 *You will follow me later.* 'To follow' Christ always carries with it the idea of costly self-offering in his cause, of martyrdom (12:24–25; Mk 8:34). Peter is thought to have been crucified in Rome about the year 65 when Nero was emperor.

37 *I will lay down my life for you.* Emotion is not an accurate measure of love as the New Testament writers understand it.

38 *Before the cock crows* ... (Mt 26:34; Mk 14:30; Lk 22:34.)

14:1 *Do not let your hearts be troubled.* The disciples had seen Jesus himself 'troubled in spirit' as he predicted the betrayal (13:21); he had spoken of his departure and said they could not come too (13:33); he had predicted Peter's denial (13:38). Things looked black. *Trust in God still.* As Jews, the disciples had been bred in the belief that however dark the outlook, God is always in control of events and 'rich in kindness and faithfulness' though it sometimes appears otherwise. *And trust in me.* Precisely the same trust is to be placed in Jesus, a trust more sure than that of the Jews because to have seen Jesus is to have seen the Father (v. 9). Below the natural fear and anxiety there can be quiet reliance upon God.

2 *There are many rooms in my Father's house.* It was a common Jewish idea of heaven, the rooms being homes. But 'home' is really a matter not of place but relationship. The true home of all men is with the Father and Jesus (v. 11).
I am going now to prepare a place for you. Jesus will open the road to the 'Father's house' by dying on the

cross, being raised from the dead, and returning to the Father. He had told the Samaritan woman of the water that he would give, 'welling up to eternal life' (4:14); his death would make him the source of life for all mankind so that they can become 'children of God' (1:12), members of his family (Mk 3:35).

3 *I shall return.* In the earliest tradition there are sayings of Jesus about the Son of Man which led the first Christians to suppose that very soon after the resurrection he would return in power and glory to establish the kingdom of God (Mk 13:26; 14:62 etc.). This was known as the Second Coming, or the Parousia (from the Greek), and all men would then be judged according to their works. John has sought to correct this idea. He has shown that judgement happens in the present as men respond to Jesus, or fail to do so (3:18–19; 5:22–29; 9:39–41). From this point in the gospel he will show that 'the return' of Jesus is a present experience.

5 *Thomas.* (11:16.)

6 *I am the Way, the Truth, and the Life.* (4:26; 6:35; 8:12, 58; 10:7, 11:11:25.) Jesus is the Way to the Father's house (v. 2), and he is the Way because he has shown how life should be lived—in self-offering to God and love of neighbour (13:5, 34). He is the Truth because he reveals in his own person the truth about God to the limit of man's capacity to understand. He is the Life because he bestows the 'life born of the Spirit' and sustains it (6:53–58).
No one can come to the Father except through me. (1:51.) Jesus is the link between God and man. Followers of other religions do not accept Christ, but where they respect his teaching as many do, they have at least seen something of his Truth.

7 *If you know me, you know my Father too.* It is the

knowledge of relationship, of personal experience.

8 *Philip.* (1:43; 6:5; 12:21.)
Let us see the Father and then we shall be satisfied.
He expressed the common difficulty, thinking in human terms as if the Father and the Son were individuals like us.

9 *To have seen me is to have seen the Father.* The one-ness of the Father and the Son is doubly underlined (v. 7) and therefore, trusting in God, the disciples must trust in Jesus whatever befalls (v. 1).

10 *I am in the Father and the Father is in me.* (10:38.)
The mutual indwelling of the Father and the Son is an important concept of which more will be heard later. For an explanation of the word 'Son' see 1:14.
The words I say to you I do not speak as from myself.
There is identity of will and purpose as between the Father and the Son (5:19).

11 *The evidence of this work.* Saving acts which are part of the whole process of redemption.

12 *Whoever believes in me will perform the same works.*
The apostles worked miracles after the resurrection and so made known the power of the Risen Christ within them (Acts 3:12–16). The vocation of most believers is not spectacular but the same force is in operation and the difference is only one of degree.
Even greater works. I.e. The conversion of the gentiles (7:35), beyond the reach of Jesus during his earthly ministry except for a few individuals (4:43–54).
Because I am going to the Father. This was the necessary preliminary to the outpouring of the Holy Spirit (7:39).

13 *Whatever you ask for in my name I will do.* This is not a promise to give us whatever we may think good and desirable. 'The name' stands for the whole

personality of the one referred to (1:12). Prayer in the name of Jesus must accord with his saving activity and follow the pattern of his prayer in Gethsemane: 'Let it be as you, not I, would have it.'

15 *If you love me you will keep my commandments.* Jesus often goes back to this point in his discourse. Real love of God lies in the steadfast endeavour to see what he requires, and then in the acceptance or performance of it. This includes self-forgetful service of others. Feelings are no guide to the measure of our love because they come and go as Peter's did (13:37–38; 18:17).

16 *Another Advocate.* The Holy Spirit (the Paraclete or Counsellor) who with and in the apostles and their successors was to proclaim the Good News throughout the world (1:33; 3:5; 7:38–39; 2:21 and note). 'Another' because Jesus himself performed the same function when he 'proclaimed the Good News from God' (Mk 1:15).

17 *The Spirit of truth.* The Holy Spirit enlightens the understanding (2:22; 12:16), leading us to Christ and the worship of the Father (4:23). St Paul speaks of him as the Spirit of God and also as the Spirit of Christ (Romans 8:9). He is personal and he is the supreme gift for which we should pray (Lk 11:13). We worship the Holy Trinity, Three Persons in One God, Father, Son, and Holy Spirit. The Holy Spirit was received after the resurrection (7:38–39; 20:22–23; Acts 2:1–13).
Whom the world cannot receive. 'The world' is indifferent or hostile to God (1:10) and therefore cannot see or know the Spirit.
He is with you, he is in you. Other versions read 'he will be in you' (20:22).

18 *I will come back to you.* (v. 3.) When the physical

presence of Jesus was withdrawn the Spirit of Christ
(v. 17) would be with them and in them.

19 *In a short time the world will no longer see me.* 'The
world' would regard his death on the cross as the
end, but the disciples would be witnesses of the
resurrection and later see him with the inward vision
of faith.

20 *On that day.* The phrase was used by Old Testament
prophets for those times when God showed clearly
that he controlled events. Here it refers to the post-
resurrection era.
I am in my Father and you in me and I in you. This
teaching, astounding as it concerns believers, is
meant to be taken as it stands and will be developed
later. St Paul's language is equally clear (Galatians
2:20; 4:19; 2 Corinthians 3:5). Born of 'water and
the Spirit' (3:5), believers are grafted into Christ at
baptism and thereafter sustained by his divine life
(4:14; 6:56; 7:38–39).

21 *Anyone who receives my commandments and keeps
them* ... (v. 15.) The love of Christ is a strenuous
enterprise involving direction of the mind and will.
The insistence on the connection between love and
obedience reflects the synoptic saying about the two
ways: 'It is a narrow gate and a hard road that leads
to life' (Mt 7:14).
I shall ... show myself to him. (v. 19.) The effort to
see and understand will be rewarded with greater
insight.

22 *Judas ... this was not Iscariot.* He was brother of
James (Lk 6:16; Acts 1:13).
*Do you intend to show yourself to us and not to the
world?* Because the Second Coming was delayed
(v. 3), it was a question which probably many people
were asking at the time when the gospel was written.

23 *If anyone loves me he will keep my word.* (v. 15.) Notice the parallel with vv. 15–16. The outcome of love expressed in keeping the commandments or word of Christ, is the continued presence of the Father and the Son with the disciple. This is the answer to the question of Judas, and the Second Coming at the end of time ceases to be a matter of urgent concern.

24 *My word is not my own.* (5:19; 7:16; 14:10.)

26 *The Holy Spirit ... will teach you ... and remind you ...* vv. 16–17.

27 *Peace I bequeath you.* 'Peace' was the conventional word of farewell, but the peace of Christ is not the mere absence of strife as understood by 'the world'. The love of the Father and the Son (vv. 15, 23) is rewarded by their continual presence which brings an interior peace, independent of external events.

28 *The Father is greater than I.* The Word was God and became man in the person of Jesus (1:1; 14:9). As man, Jesus speaks of the Father as greater than himself (5:19).

30 *The prince of this world.* (12:31.)

31 *Come now, let us go.* The words are paralleled in Mt 26:46//Mk 14:42, and come after the agony in Gethsemane and just before the arrest of Jesus. Here they are followed by two more chapters of teaching and the priestly prayer in ch. 17. They connect well with the beginning of ch. 18 and it has been suggested that chs. 15–17 were not part of the original gospel but were added later. On the other hand the words can be interpreted as Christ's invitation to the embryonic Church to look at the dangers to be faced in following in the steps of his Passion, and to consider the grounds of its strength.

The true vine

In the Old Testament the vine is the symbol for the
Israel of God (Isaiah 5:1–7), chosen to be 'a kingdom
of priests, a consecrated nation' (Exodus 19:6).
Throughout her history however, Israel had been
stubborn and disobedient except for a faithful few,
and she failed when faced with the supreme test of
being required to recognise Jesus as the Messiah
(Mk 12:1–9). The vine did not bear fruit.

15:1 *I am the true vine.* (4:26; 6:35; 8:12, 58; 10:7,
11; 11:25; 14:6.) Jesus is the true vine because he
sums up in himself all that Israel was meant to be
and to do. He is the true vine also because he is the
source from which the cup at every Eucharist is
filled (2:2–8; 6:53–54; Mk 14:23–24).

2 *Every branch in me* ... Sap from the main stem
flows to every branch. The divine life is in all the
disciples (14:20, 23), but, never over-ruling the
individual will, is no magical guarantee against
failure in keeping Christ's commandments.
(*The branch*) *that bears no fruit.* Even in the first
century there were break-away groups that formed
separate congregations. The reference is probably to
these.

3 *You are pruned already.* The washing of the feet
(13:10) should perhaps be understood as representing the change in the disciples which their association
with Jesus had brought about.

4 *Make your home in me, as I make mine in you.* With
the courage which the knowledge of this mutual
indwelling would give, and with his gift of peace
(14:27), the apostles would be equipped for their
mission to the world (14:31).

5 *Fruit in plenty.* The fruit must not be understood as
success as the world sees it. Trust in Christ (14:1)

187

implies response to his direction, and only he knows the particular objective. For the qualities which are the fruit of the Spirit see Galatians 5:22–24.

6 *Anyone who does not remain in me ... withers.* If the divine life is indeed a reality, 'the branch' which separates must of necessity 'wither'.
These branches ... are burnt. We are God's creatures, made to find fulfilment and joy in him. Utter loss is the inevitable result of breaking relationship with him.

7 *If you remain in me ... you may ask what you will.* Because the will of the believer is at one with the will of Christ (14:13).

10 *If you keep my commandments ...* The point is hammered home (14:15, 21, 23).

11 *My own joy ... your joy.* Joy is the outcome of harmony.

12 *Love one another, as I have loved you.* The extent of Christ's love is to be seen on the cross and the words seem to imply that the crucifixion has already taken place.

15 *I call you friends, because I have made known to you everything ...* The obedience of the disciples grows from trust and is freely rendered. The openness of friendship is therefore possible for Jesus.

16 *I chose you; and I commissioned you.* Jesus chose the disciples early in his ministry and the synoptic gospels tell how he sent them out on missionary journeys (Mt 10:5–16; Mk 6:7–13; Lk 9:1–6). The final commission was given after the resurrection (Jn 20:21–23; Mt 28:18–20; Acts 1:1–8). The apostles had a special commission, but every disciple called out of 'the world' is required to be true to the particular vocation laid upon him (v. 5).

Fruit that will last. There is no doubt as to the result of the Church's mission (16:33).

The hostile world

18 *If the world hates you, remember ...* The love of the disciples for one another is contrasted with the hatred which they face together. They are at one with Christ and therefore hatred of them is hatred of him (2:21).

21 *They will do all this because they do not know the one who sent me.* They cannot know God if they do not acknowledge him in Jesus.

22 *Their sin.* Sin is the deliberate rejection of the light. The Jews had listened to the teaching of Jesus and seen his works, but they did not want to accept the clear evidence (5:31–47).

25 *All this was only to fulfil the words written ...* (10:35; 12:38; 13:18.) The quotation is from Psalm 35:19.

26 *The Spirit ... will be my witness. And you too ...* The Church exists to witness to Christ, beginning from the fact of the resurrection (Acts 1:15–22). It will be remembered that John's purpose in writing the gospel was to show exactly what must be proclaimed about Jesus (Introduction D.).
Because you have been with me from the outset. What the apostles had to say was not based on hearsay, but on first-hand evidence (Acts 1:21–22).

16:1 *They will expel you from the synagogues.* The first Christians regarded themselves as a reforming movement within Judaism. They were expelled from the synagogues for witnessing to Christ and neglecting the ritual law of Moses.
Anyone who kills you ... Saul, afterwards St Paul is an outstanding example of this (Acts 7:55–60).

4 *I have told you all this ...* Early in his discourse
(14:1) Jesus had told the disciples that they must put
the same trust in him as in the Father. Persecution
would test that trust to the uttermost.

The coming of the Advocate

7 *Unless I go, the Advocate will not come to you.* (7:39;
15:26–27.)

8 *When he comes, he will show the world how wrong it
was.* His coming would be as important for 'the
world' as for the disciples. Its error in regard to
Jesus would be sharply exposed.

9 *About sin: proved by their refusal to believe in me.*
(15:22.) The Jews are representative of 'the world'
because the ministry of Jesus was largely confined
to them, but their attitude is characteristic of all
mankind.

10 *About who was in the right: proved by my going to the
Father.* The Advocate would make 'the world' see
that the resurrection of Jesus and his return to the
Father was God's victory and the means whereby he
accomplished the salvation of all mankind.

11 *About judgement.* 'The world' would be made to
recognise that the death of Jesus had broken the
power of the devil by showing what love is, and by
making his life available to believers. It would acknowledge that it had been wrong.

13 *The Spirit ... will lead you to the complete truth.* The
words and acts of Jesus are the words and acts of
God. It is the function of the Spirit to call them to
remembrance and shed light upon them.
He will tell you of the things to come. The death and
resurrection of Jesus, and his return to the Father,
make operative in the present the final judgement

(vv. 9–11) expected at the end of history, 'the things to come' (14:3).

14 *He will glorify me.* The return in glory at the Last Day will be seen to have been anticipated by the resurrection.

15 *Everything the Father has is mine* ... Jesus reveals the glory of the Father, and the Holy Spirit leads us to the truth of the revelation (v. 13).

Jesus to return very soon

16 *A short time later you will see me again.* In the context of the last supper the words refer to his appearances after the resurrection. They also refer to the Second Coming (14:3).

20 *The world will rejoice.* (15:18.)

21 *A woman in childbirth suffers.* It was a common Jewish metaphor for the troubles which were expected to precede the coming of the Son of Man in glory (Mk 13:7–8, 24–27). Jesus had told Nicodemus that a man had to be born from above if he was to see the kingdom of God (3:3), and St Paul writes of 'the new self created in God's way'. Jesus seems to be predicting the joy the apostles will experience when they see the changed lives of their converts. Remaining in the vine (15:4) and bearing fruit, their joy would be complete (15:11).

23 *When that day comes, you will not ask me any questions.* In the post-resurrection era they would have the Spirit to lead them to the complete truth.
Ask ... from the Father ... in my name. (14:13.)

25 *I shall ... tell you about the Father in plain terms.* John represents the disciples as having recognised Jesus as the Messiah from the outset (1:41; 6:69), but it was only after the resurrection and with the

191

Spirit to guide them that they would grasp the whole truth. This truth would greatly enrich the knowledge of God which they had had before the coming of Christ.

29 *His disciples said, 'Now you are speaking plainly ... we see ...'* They meant well, like Peter (13:37–38), and Jesus dealt with them in the same way.

32 *The time will come ... when you will be scattered.* (Mk 14:27.)

33 *I have conquered the world.* (vv. 8–11.) Again there is the implication that the crucifixion lies in the past (15:12, 16).

The priestly prayer of Christ

There are frequent references in the gospels to the prayers of Jesus, but in only four instances are we given their substance. He prayed for Simon that his faith might not fail (Lk 22:32). He prayed before raising Lazarus from the dead, the brief expression of the continuous communion with the Father. He prayed in Gethsemane before his Passion (Mt 26:36–46; Mk 14:32–42; Lk 22:40–46), and finally there is the priestly prayer in Jn. In this gospel the Gethsemane prayer is omitted, but in chs. 14–16 its lesson in obedience is strongly emphasised. 'Let it be as you, not I, would have it' is the heart of the prayer. The priestly prayer, like that other, is placed just before the arrest. In it we see the divine Son in serene communion with the Father, praying for the apostles and those who would believe through them. The clear literary form of the prayer suggests that as it stands, it was the work of John. But that does not rule out the possibility of there being a genuine tradition behind it. Jesus was God and man and his prayer before his Passion may well have found different modes of expression.

In the post-resurrection era the apostles were aware of the presence of Jesus with them. It was natural to believe that in his continuous creative activity, he still prayed for them (Romans 8:4; Hebrews 7:25). The priestly prayer then, is to be understood not only in the immediate context of the Passion, but as a reminder to the Church for all time that Christ lives 'for ever to intercede for all who come to God through him'.

17:1 *The hour has come.* (2:4; 7:6, 30; 12:23, 27.)
Glorify your Son so that your Son may glorify you. (13:31–32.) The Father glorifies the Son by raising him from the dead and taking him to himself in glory. The judgement of 'the world' is thus proved wrong (16:9–11), and the love clearly revealed which achieved our salvation. Thus the Son glorifies the Father.

3 *Eternal life is this*: *to know you* ... Eternal life consists in a living relationship with the Father, and Jesus Christ who fully reveals him (14:7, 9).

6 *I have made your name known.* The thought now turns to the disciples. For the force of 'name' see 1:12; 14:13–14.
The men you took from the world to give me. (15:16.) *They have kept your word.* The apostles have proclaimed the Good News that to be 'in Jesus' is to have eternal life.

10 *In them I am glorified.* Caught up and included in the love of the Father for the Son, and of the Son for the Father, the apostles show forth the glory of the Son because in the strength of his life they 'bear fruit, fruit that will last' (15:16).

11 *Holy Father.* To the Hebrews the essential characteristic of holiness was separateness. God inspired reverential awe because he was so utterly distinct

from his creatures. If the apostles were to be true to his name, they would have to acquire something of that separateness—in the world but not of it.

That they may be one. The apostles are to be made one by the holiness which they all derive from the Father and the Son, and as one to make manifest the eternal glory of God. There is to be 'one flock, and one shepherd' (10:16).

12 *The one who chose to be lost.* His fate was not decided before ever he was born. He made his choice of his own free will.

To fulfil the scriptures. Psalm 41:9, quoted at 13:18.

13 *To share my joy with them.* (15:11.)

17 *Consecrate them in the truth.* Jesus is the Truth, the revelation of the Father and his saving love. Grounded in this faith, the apostles are set apart from the world to take the Good News to it at whatever cost to themselves.

18 *As you sent me into the world, I have sent them.* (15:16.) 'Apostolos' was the Greek word for 'ambassador', someone with full authority to act for the sender. Having received their commission (20:21), the disciples became apostles.

19 *For their sake I consecrate myself.* A priest in the Temple would make a solemn preparation both of himself and the victim, before offering sacrifice. Jesus prepares as both priest and victim for the cross. *So that they too may be consecrated.* By the gift of the Holy Spirit they would be able to follow Jesus in self-offering.

20 *I pray . . . for those also who through their words will believe in me.* The prayer now moves outwards to include the multitudes who, through the centuries, would be brought into the Church.

21 *That they may be one in us.* The members of the
    Church, living and no longer in this life, are one
    family in the household of the Father and the Son.
    So that the world may believe ... The Church exists
    to fulfil a mission to the world because God 'sent the
    Son ... that the world through him might be saved'
    (3:17).

22 *I have given them the glory you gave me.* The Church
    is in Christ, living on his life (15:1), and must there-
    fore share in his obedience and suffering which is his
    glory, the revelation of his love.
    That they may be one as we are one. The subject of
    unity, introduced at v. 11, is strongly emphasised in
    vv. 21–23. There were divisions in the Church even
    in the first century and it is much divided now al-
    though there has been a steady move towards unity
    in the last decades. Disunity weakens the effective-
    ness of its mission. (10:16).

24 *Father, I want those you have given me to be with me.*
    There is no difference in the will and desire of the
    Father and the Son. It is a statement of a common
    purpose.

25 *Father, Righteous One.* Old Testament kings sat in
    judgement, deciding on the rights and wrongs of the
    cases brought before them. The righteous king was
    the one whose just decisions brought liberation. God
    has pronounced the world to be wrong in its rejection
    of Christ (16:9–11) and thereby brought liberation
    to his people.

26 *So that the love with which you loved me may be in
    them.* 'True' love must be essentially the same,
    regardless of its object. Jesus is the perfect revelation
    of the Father and therefore in his love for mankind is
    to be found the nature of the love of the Father for
    the Son. Love is concerned to give and not to get:

'God loved the world so much that he gave' (3:16).
The giving is costly; 'he gave his only Son', and his
Son died for us. I Corinthians 13 is the classic
exposition of the subject.

C. THE PASSION

The gospel has taught that Jesus, the Word made
flesh, brought a fresh dimension of life into the
world distinct from our ordinary natural life (3:5–6).
Six signs have been described showing his life-giving
power, and pointing to his divine Sonship. Now in
the seventh, we are to be told how that life was to be
made available for all men everywhere, and for ever.
Differences from the synoptic accounts may be
partly due to the use of different traditions. They
can also be accounted for by John's primary purpose
which was to show the real significance of the
separate events within the Passion Narrative.

The arrest of Jesus (Mt 26:47–56; Mk 14:43–50;
Lk 22:47–53)

18:1 *Jesus left with his disciples.* (14:31.) He left the house
where the supper had taken place.
(*He*) *crossed the Kedron valley.* (Jn only.) It lies to
the east of Jerusalem with the Mount of Olives on the
far side.
There was a garden there. In Mt 26:36//Mk 14:32,
Jesus took the disciples to a small estate called
Gethsemane, and in Lk he went as usual to the
Mount of Olives. John again mentions a garden
(19:41) as 'the place where they crucified him' and
where too was the tomb where they laid him.
Readers whose scriptures were the Old Testament
would be reminded of the garden where Adam and
Eve brought sin into the world through their dis-

obedience (Genesis 3). Now in this other garden, Jesus through his obedience reversed that disaster.

2 *Judas knew the place well.* People came in such numbers to Jerusalem for the Passover that many camped out for lack of other accommodation. Judas knew where Jesus was most likely to be found.

3 *He brought the cohort to this place.* (Jn only.) A cohort numbered six hundred men, a huge number for the arrest of Jesus and eleven disciples. If the governor had been warned of the supposed claims of Jesus, he might have decided to take precautions against strong popular support. But in that case Jesus would have been taken directly before the governor, and not the high priest. It seems likely that a theological point is being made; Jesus faced the hostile world (15:18).

A detachment of guards. These were Temple police, a Jewish force under the control of the Sanhedrin. And these were in addition to the cohort.

With lanterns and torches and weapons. Passover always comes at full moon and the trees in the garden would hardly provide effective cover from a whole cohort supported by a detachment of guards. The feeble lights and weapons of 'the world' are useless against the 'light that shines in the darkness' (1:5), against Jesus who has 'conquered the world' (16:33).

4 *Knowing everything ... Jesus then came forward.* He advanced because 'his hour' appointed by the Father had come, and not to counter the threat. He has 'power over all mankind' (17:2), and when he lays down his life it will be of his own free will (10:18; Mt 26:53).

5 *I am he.* He is Jesus the Nazarene. He is also I AM (12:58).

Judas the traitor was standing among them. (v. 2.)

He stands with 'the world'. There is no mention of
his kiss (Mt 26:49; Mk 14:45; Lk 22:47).

6 *They moved back and fell to the ground.* They were
overwhelmed by his majesty and authority and
unable to do anything he did not allow.

8 *If I am the one you are looking for, let these others go.*
He is the good shepherd 'who lays down his life for
the sheep' (10:11).

9 *Not one of those you gave me have I lost.* (6:39;
10:28; 17:12.)

10 *Simon Peter, who carried a sword.* The names indicate
a later, not an earlier tradition (6:5). All the gospels
mention swords being carried, something forbidden
once Passover had started. This accords with John's
dating of the crucifixion (see note introducing ch. 13).
His right ear. (Lk 22:50.) The healing is only mentioned in Lk.

11 *Am I not to drink the cup the Father has given me?*
The words recall the Gethsemane prayer omitted by
John (Mt 26:39; Mk 14:36; Lk 22:42). The cup
was the Old Testament symbol both of suffering and
of joy. He suffered to conquer, and from that victory
springs our joy (16:22).

Jesus before Annas and Caiaphas. Peter disowns him
(Mt 26:57–75; Mk 14:53–73; Lk 22:47–65)

12 *The cohort . . . and the Jewish guards seized Jesus and
bound him.* The size of the force sent to arrest him
and the bonds suggest the complete futility of 'the
world' in its efforts to overcome the Word made
flesh, 'a light that darkness could not overpower'
(1:5). In Mt//Mk Jesus was bound at the orders of
the Sanhedrin before being taken to Pilate. Luke
makes no mention of bonds.

13 *They took him first to Annas.* Annas was high priest from A.D. 6 to 15 when he was deposed by the Romans. He is mentioned in Lk 3:2 as being in office during the Baptist's ministry about 27.
Caiaphas . . . high priest that year. (11:49–52.) He was continuously in office from 18–36 but Annas seems to have retained considerable influence. It is only here that we are told that Annas was father-in-law of Caiaphas.

15 *Simon Peter, with another disciple, followed Jesus.* (Mt 26:58; Mk 14:54; Lk 22:54.) Only John mentions the second disciple, often identified with the one Jesus loved (13:23) though with no real grounds for doing so.
This disciple . . . was known to the high priest. The high priest was a Jerusalem aristocrat. If the disciple was indeed John Zebedee, the fisherman's son from Galilee, it is difficult to see how the connection could have been established.

17 *The maid on duty at the door.* (Mt 26:69–75; Mk 14:66–72; Lk 22:54–62.) The story is told in very precise terms. Who the speakers were is made clear (v. 10).
He answered, 'I am not'. There is no mention of Peter's oaths. The denial is deliberate and cold. Like Judas (v. 5) Peter has ranged himself with 'the world'. Jesus is alone.

19 *The high priest questioned Jesus.* In the synoptic gospels, the preliminary hearing was before members of the Sanhedrin assembled in the high priest's house. Here the high priest appears to have been alone except for the guards. He represents the established religion.
About his disciples and his teaching. The real charge against Jesus was of blasphemy. He had called God his Father (5:17–18; 10:22–23). The penalty for

199

blasphemy was death, and death had already been decided upon (11:47–53).

20 *I have spoken openly ... in the synagogue and the Temple.* Jesus, the Light and the Truth, exposed the falsity of the proceedings. See the synoptic account of his challenge to the rabble which came to arrest him (Mt 26:55; Mk 14:49; Lk 22:53).

22 *One of the guards ... gave Jesus a slap on the face.* Note the economy in description as contrasted with Mk 14:64–65. The words of Jesus to the guard emphasise the grossness of the injustice being done.

24 *Then Annas sent him ... to Caiaphas.* This is a puzzling statement. Vv. 15, 19, imply that the hearing had been before Caiaphas. It has been suggested that the text suffered displacement perhaps owing to a scribal error and that v. 24 should follow immediately after v. 14. We should then read that after his arrest Jesus was taken to Annas who sent him, still bound, to Caiaphas.

27 *Again Peter denied it; and at once a cock crew.* (13:38.) Peter's recall of the Lord's prophecy and his own bitter tears have no place here. What was three times stated was always understood as final and confirmed. Peter disowned Christ completely.

Jesus before Pilate (Mt 27:2, 11–26; Mk 15:1–15; Lk 23:1–7, 13–25)

28 *The Praetorium.* This was the governor's official residence in Jerusalem. Pilate lived mostly at Caesarea, a predominantly heathen town on the coast, because it was necessary for the Romans to keep a low profile in the Holy City. At Passover however, when riots were likely he had to be at hand.

It was now morning. All the gospels agree that Jesus

was taken before Pilate early in the morning following the night of his arrest.

They did not go into the Praetorium. (Jn only.) Their
values are being exposed; sensitive about ritual
defilement incurred by going into a heathen place,
they saw nothing wrong about plotting a murder.
The detail is historically important because it is
consistent with John's dating of the crucifixion
(13:1).

30 *If he were not a criminal* . . . The real charge against
Jesus (11:45–51) is not mentioned. Mt 27:11//Mk
15:2 show Pilate as being aware of the main accusation from the outset. In Lk 23:2 Jesus was accused
of inciting to revolt, opposing payment of tribute,
and claiming to be Christ, a king.

31 *Try him by your own law.* Pilate was well aware that
'it was out of jealousy they had handed him over'
(Mt 27:18; Mk 15:10).

We are not allowed to put a man to death. They
appeared to be able to stone to death for blasphemy
(8:59; 10:31) and the fact of having gone to Pilate
would have made it obvious to him that there were
political factors involved.

32 *This was to fulfil the words Jesus had spoken* . . .
(3:14; 8:28; 12:32, 34.)

33 *So Pilate . . . called Jesus to him.* Jesus entered the
Praetorium leaving his accusers outside.

Are you the king of the Jews? (Mt 27:11; Mk 15:2;
Lk 23:3.) The title 'Christ' was beyond the comprehension of the gentile foreigner and 'king' was the
best substitute. The question is very important in Jn
because the whole gospel was designed to explain the
identity of Jesus of Nazareth; it will be shown that
it was as king he was condemned (19:15), crucified

(19:19), and reigns universally from the cross (19:20; 12:32).

34 *Do you ask this of your own accord ... ?* If it was prompted by personal interest it might be the beginning of discipleship (1:38). Otherwise it was just an official inquiry.

35 *Am I a Jew?* Romans were generally contemptuous of the bitter wrangles on religious matters characteristic of the Jews and Pilate probably wondered at the strength of the hatred that had brought Jesus where he was.

36 *Mine is not a kingdom of this world.* Not only the person of the King (v. 33) but the nature of his kingdom has been a main theme of the gospel. It has no boundaries (4:42); its subjects are born of the Spirit (3:6); children in the household of God (1:12; 11:52; 14:2).
My men would have fought. (Mt 26:52–53.)

37 *It is you who say it.* I.e. 'The words are yours' (Mt 27:11; Mk 15:2; Lk 23:3). Pilate could not be expected to understand the kingship of Jesus. *I was born for this, I came into the world for this.* There is the distinction here between the human and the divine. He was born as man and his birth was the coming of the eternal Word into human history.
To bear witness to the truth. (14:6.)

38 *I find no case against him.* (Mt 27:23; Mk 15:14; Lk 23:4.)

39 *A custom of yours.* (Mt 27:15–18; Mk 15:6–14; Lk 23:18–23.) Outside the gospels there is no contemporary evidence for this custom.

40 '*Not this man*', *they said*, '*but Barabbas*'. The name means 'son of the father'. The original party led by

Caiaphas, now joined by a crowd, rejected the Son of the Father and demanded the other, the brigand.

19:1 *Pilate then had Jesus scourged.* As a rule scourging immediately preceded execution (Mt 27:26; Mk 15:15). John seems to suggest that Pilate tried to move the Jews to compassion.

2 *Thorns into a crown ... a purple robe.* (Mt 27:27–31; Mk 15:16-20.) The soldiers mocked Jesus as a make-believe king, degrading his royalty to the lowest depth. In Lk this was done by Herod's soldiers (Lk 23:11).
They slapped him in the face. (18:22.)

4 *Pilate came outside again.* (18:29, 38.) The scourging and the mockery took place in the soldiers quarters within the Praetorium and Pilate had withdrawn meanwhile.
Look, I am going to bring him out to you to let you see. The Baptist had urged the people to look (1:29, 36), and in his own way John had been urging his readers to do the same.
Here is the man. Humiliated, lacerated, outcast and alone, Jesus stands identified with all the misery of mankind (Mt 25:35–36, 40). He is also the divine Son, God himself, who by that identification with man takes away the sin of the world (1:29: Isaiah 53:1–9). Unwittingly Pilate points to his eternal sovereignty (16:33).

6 *Take him yourselves and crucify him.* It was a taunt.

7 *We have a Law.* (Leviticus 24:16.) 'The one who blasphemes the name of Yahweh must die' (18:31).
He has claimed to be the Son of God. The real charge is made at last. The Jews express the truth which John set out to teach.

8 *(Pilate's) fears increased.* Politically Pilate's position

was awkward. He could expect riots if he acquitted a man the Sanhedrin was determined to get rid of, and then questions from Rome. But something about the personality of Jesus made him very uneasy too (Mt 27:19).

9 *Where do you come from?* Earlier, Pilate had wanted to know who Jesus was (18:33). Now he asks a second question to which the gospel has given the answer, and which the Jews have continued to ask (6:42; 7:27, 41; 8:19).
Jesus made no answer. The silence of Jesus during the trials is not emphasised here as in the synoptic gospels.

11 *You would have no power over me* ... Pilate derived his authority from the Roman Emperor, but he in his turn only had authority because God allowed him to have it (Romans 13:1).
The one who handed me over to you has the greater guilt. Probably Caiaphas is meant. Judas was only a tool in the hands of the Jewish authorities and it is to them that the real responsibility for the crucifixion is being ascribed.

Jesus is condemned to death

12 *Pilate was anxious to set him free.* This was established in the tradition at a very early date (Acts 3:13–14).
If you set him free you are no friend of Caesar's. Jesus, as a false Messiah, might head a rebellion against the Romans (10:38).

13 *A place called the Pavement.* It was an open air tribunal, necessary because the Jews would not enter the Praetorium. It is not mentioned elsewhere.
In Hebrew Gabbatha. A satisfactory interpretation of the name has never been found. The place has not been identified.

14 *It was Passover Preparation Day*. (13:1; 18:28.)
Everything had to be prepared in advance so that the
rest enjoined by the Law at Passover should not be
broken.
About the sixth hour. About noon (4:6). By that time
all leaven, the symbol of evil, had to be removed from
the houses. Only unleavened bread might be eaten
during the feast (Exodus 12:15; I Corinthians 5:7).

15 *We have no king but Caesar*. It was a denial of their
faith. God was their king and their monarchs had
only been his deputies. Now they acclaimed a gentile
foreigner in place of God. Jesus had said, 'Those
who reject me reject the one who sent me' (Lk
10:16; Jn 5:23; 12:48).

The crucifixion (Mt 27:32–56; Mk 15:21–41; Lk
23:33–49)

17 *They then took charge of Jesus*. I.e. the Roman
soldiers.
Carrying his own cross. If John knew the tradition
about Simon of Cyrene (Mt 27:32; Mk 15:21; Lk
23:26) he preferred not to use it. Jesus was in full
control and needed no help (10:18; 18:4).
The place of the skull ... in Hebrew Golgotha. (Mt
27:33; Mk 15:22; Lk 23:33.) In this gospel, a
garden (19:41).

18 *They crucified him with two others ... Jesus in the
middle*. (Mt 27:38; Mk 15:27; Lk 23:32–33.)
Nothing is said here about the mockery to which he
was subjected as he hung on the cross.

19 *Pilate wrote out a notice*. (Mt 27:37; Mk 15:26; Lk
23:38.) It was usual to inform the public by this
means of the reason for the execution.
Jesus the Nazarene, King of the Jews. The other
evangelists mention the notice and immediately pass
on to other matters, but here great emphasis is laid

205

upon it. The Son of Man is lifted up and glorified, showing how much God loves the world (3:16). Jesus reigns from the cross.

20 *The writing was in Hebrew, Latin and Greek.* (Jn only.) It was in Hebrew because Jesus was the culmination of the experience and history of Israel, the Chosen People of God (Exodus 19:6); in Latin because that was the official language of the Roman Empire, the known world to the readers of the gospel; in Greek because it was the language in common use throughout the civilised parts of the Empire. Jesus is Sovereign and Saviour of the world (4:42).

22 *What I have written, I have written.* The statement was made and it would stand. Pilate was a gentile who did not understand Judaism or believe in Jesus, but he had witnessed to the truth.

Christ's garments divided

23 *The soldiers ... took his clothing.* (Mt 27:35; Mk 15:24; Lk 23:34.) The sharing out of the garments of the crucified was customary procedure, the ultimate deprivation and humiliation.
His undergarment was seamless. (Jn only.) Jesus had offered his prayer as high priest before his arrest and this was the hour of sacrifice (17:19). The high priest's tunic was seamless 'woven in one piece'. From a very early period the seamless tunic has symbolised the unity of 'the scattered children of God' (10:16; 11:52).

24 *The words of scripture were fulfilled.* (Psalm 22:18.) The whole psalm has always been valued for its relevance to the Passion Narrative. The gentile soldiers, caught up like Pilate in a stupendous event beyond their capacity to imagine or understand,

like him played their part in bringing out its significance.

Jesus and his mother (Jn only)

25 *Near the cross of Jesus stood his mother.* (2:1.) In the
other gospels women are mentioned as watching
from a distance (Mt 27:55–56; Mk 15:40–41; Lk
23:49). It seems unlikely that in actual fact they
would have been allowed close to the cross.
His mother's sister. This may have been Salome,
mother of James and John Zebedee (Mk 15:40; Mt
27:56), or the phrase may refer to what follows,
'Mary, the wife of Clopas'. Clopas may have been
the Cleopas of Lk 24:18. *Mary of Magdala.* Her
name is included in this context by both Matthew
and Mark. She had been cured of demon possession
early in the Galilean ministry (Lk 8:2), and was
early identified though without real grounds, with
the woman who was a sinner (Lk 7:36–50), as well
as with Mary the sister of Lazarus.

26 *The disciple he loved.* (13:23.)
Woman, this is your son. Jesus was in extremity but
could still think of his mother and what should be
done for her. For the tradition see Introduction A.
By the time the gospel was written the Church had
severed all links with Judaism. Possibly to John, the
episode suggested that the breach was contrary to
the will of Christ, his mother representing the Old
Israel from which he took his humanity and the
disciple the New Israel, the Church, each being
consigned to the care of the other.

The death of Jesus

28 *Jesus knew that everything had been completed.* The
mission of salvation which he, the Word made flesh,
had come to accomplish, was completed. His death

was quiet and serene. Two psalms (22, 69) which have always been regarded as pre-figuring the crucifixion, begin in agony and end in praise and thanksgiving. We can understand the tradition contained in Mt//Mk (Mt 27:45–46; Mk 15:33–34) which includes the darkness and the cry of desolation as telling us part of what happened while in Jn we have the other, Lk combining elements from both.

I am thirsty. (Jn only.) Thirst was one of the special tortures of crucifixion (Psalm 22:15; 69:21; Jn 4:7).

29 *A jar full of vinegar.* (Mt 27:48; Mk 15:36.) It was sour wine which the soldiers had with them.

A hyssop stick. Hyssop is a bushy, aromatic plant. On the night of the first Passover, hyssop dipped in the blood of lambs slain for the feast, was used to daub every Israelite house as a sign to the destroying angel to pass over it (Exodus 12:22–23). In Mt//Mk the sponge was put on a reed which would seem more practical, but the Crucified was probably not lifted far from the ground and it would be possible to reach with the hyssop. The association of hyssop with the Passover was an important detail of course to John (13:1).

30 *It is accomplished.* It is the Victor's shout of triumph. He had revealed the love of God for man, and shown what man ought to be. His life was at the point of release to become the true life of all men (15:2, 4).

He gave up his spirit. He gave it up. It was not taken from him (10:18; 18:4; 19:17). The synoptists make the same statement.

The pierced Christ (Jn only)

31 *It was Preparation Day.* (18:28; 19:14.) As Passover and the sabbath coincided that year it was specially important that the Law enjoining the removal of the bodies of the crucified from their crosses before

nightfall, should be observed (Deuteronomy 21:23). *The Jews asked Pilate to have the legs broken.* Death was sometimes long in coming and was hastened by this means. The body sagged so that normal breathing became impossible.

33 *Jesus . . . was already dead.* No bone of the Passover lamb might be broken (v. 36; Exodus 12:46).

34 *One of the soldiers pierced his side.* The soldiers were under orders to execute the condemned and failure to do so meant paying the penalty themselves. All the evangelists stress the actuality of the death because if Jesus did not really die as some people tried to maintain, he was not raised from the dead and we are 'still in our sins' (I Corinthians 15:17).
Blood and water. Life and unreserved offering to God; life and cleansing. This is the culminating point of a theme introduced in the first chapter of the gospel and continued throughout. Jesus is the new Sanctuary replacing the old Temple (2:19), the source of true life and cleansing, particularly as given in the two great sacraments of the Church, Baptism and the Eucharist. He is thus the means of our salvation (1:16; 3:5; 4:14; 6:56; 7:37; 15:4).

35 *This is the evidence of one who saw it.* The subject of witness was also introduced at the very beginning of the gospel and constantly returned to. It is brought in here with tremendous emphasis. It was either the author himself who saw, or someone in whom he had absolute confidence, the disciple Jesus loved perhaps.

36 *Not one bone of his will be broken.* (v. 33.) Two texts have been combined, Exodus 12:46 and Psalm 34:20.

37 *They will look on the one whom they have pierced.* (Zechariah 12:10.) The prophet was referring to a great public figure, probably a priest-king of the second century B.C. who was struck down by an

assassin and mourned by the nation 'as for an only son'. John saw the Jews as coming to an understanding of Christ's death, and so to penitence and belief.

The burial (Mt 27:57–60; Mk 15:42–46; Lk 23:50–54)

38 *Joseph of Arimathaea*. Not previously mentioned by John, he was a prominent member of the Sanhedrin, one of many secret disciples (12:42).
Pilate gave permission (for the removal of the body).
An official permit had to be obtained before bodies could be removed after crucifixion. It was important to have documentary evidence that death had taken place and that permission for removal had been received.

39 *Nicodemus came as well.* (3:1–10; 7:50–52.)
A mixture of myrrh and aloes, weighing a hundred pounds. The body was 'bound with bands of stuff' (11:44), the spices being placed within the layers. It was all quite usual except for the quantity of spices which was enormous. Only John tells of the linen cloths; the synoptists speak of a shroud.

41 *At a place where he had been crucified there was a garden.* (18:1.)

42 *Since it was the Jewish Day of Preparation ...* (18:28; 19:14, 31.) There was no time to spare and the tomb was conveniently at hand, prepared by Joseph for his own use (Mt 27:60). They appear to have laid the body of Jesus there as a temporary arrangement until after the feast when a permanent burial place could be found.

VIII. THE DAY OF CHRIST'S RESURRECTION

The empty tomb (Mt 28:1–8; Mk 16:1–8; Lk 24:1–11)

20:1 *Very early on the first day of the week.* It was before dawn on the Sunday, always described as the third day after the crucifixion (I Corinthians 5:4) because the Jews included the first and last number of a sequence in their reckoning.

Mary of Magdala came to the tomb. (19:25.) She was alone according to John but the other gospels tell of other women being with her. Her object in going to the tomb must have been simply 'to weep there' (11:31) since there was nothing practical left for her to do (cf. Mk 16:1; Lk 24:1).

She saw that the stone had been moved away. Mt//Mk explain that the entrance to the tomb was blocked with a great stone after the body of Jesus had been placed inside. Here as in Lk, the fact that it had been removed by the morning is all that is said.

2 *Simon Peter and the other disciple.* (18:15.)

They have taken the Lord out of the tomb. She appears to have thought that Joseph of Arimathaea and Nicodemus had taken action during the night. Notice how the synoptic tradition seems to have been assimilated to this one. She speaks as if she had companions.

3 *Peter set out . . . to go to the tomb.* (Lk 24:12.)

5 (*The other disciple*) *bent down.* The entrance was low and the body would have been placed down one side. He could not see without stooping.

(*He*) *did not go in.* Possibly dawning understanding and reverence made him hold back (v. 8), or he may simply have deferred to Peter as an older man and leader among the disciples.

6 *The linen cloths on the ground* ... They had been left like a shell (cf. 11:44).

8 *The other disciple saw* ... *and he believed.* The connection between seeing and believing is a theme running through the whole gospel and culminating in the worship of Thomas (19:34–35). The disciple did not see Jesus, only the empty tomb and the linen cloths lying. He understood the seventh and greatest sign. He knew that Jesus was the Son of God.

9 *The teaching of scripture.* (Psalm 16:6–11.) The first Christians searched the scriptures for precise predictions about the life, death and resurrection of Jesus, and made a collection. This Psalm was one of their important texts. In these days the value of the Old Testament is found in its whole teaching about the character, purposes and activity of God, and the coming of Christ and his way of salvation is seen to be entirely consistent with it.

The appearance to Mary of Magdala (Jn only)

11 *She stooped to look inside.* It was simply because she saw the stone had been moved that she went to fetch the disciples (v. 1). She had not looked inside before.

12 *Two angels in white sitting.* In Mk a 'young man in a white robe' was seated inside the tomb. In Lk 'two men in brilliant white clothes' suddenly appeared. In Mt the angel of the Lord descended from heaven and rolled away the stone. The presence of the angels indicates that a mighty act of God is the explanation for the empty tomb.

13 *They have taken my Lord away* ... (v. 2.) She did not recognise the angels for what they were, or expect them to know anything about her.

14 *She did not recognise (Jesus).* There seems to have been a change in Jesus after the resurrection: he was not always immediately recognised (Jn 21:4; Lk 24:15–16; Mt 28:17).

15 *Supposing him to be the gardener.* The Risen Lord blended with the circumstances in which he was encountered. He was not alarming or startling in any way.
Who are you looking for? As so often in the gospels, Jesus asked a question so leading to the truth.

16 *Jesus said, 'Mary!' She knew him then and said ... 'Rabbuni!'* The Good Shepherd calls his own sheep 'one by one' and they follow him 'because they know his voice' (10:3–4, 14, 27). 'Rabbuni' was the form of the word 'Rabbi' used almost exclusively in address to God.

17 *Do not cling to me.* She was clasping his feet (Mt 28:10).
Because I have not yet ascended to the Father. This is difficult as it stands because his return to the Father meant the withdrawal of his physical presence. It seems clear however that the disciples must get used to the idea that their relationship with the Lord will be different when they can no longer see, hear, or touch him.
Go and find the brothers, and tell them ... (Mt 28:10; Lk 24:9.)
I am ascending to my Father. Luke represented the return of Jesus to the glory of the Father as a physical going up into heaven because heaven was always imagined as being 'up there'. John has generally preferred to speak of Jesus as going to, or returning to the Father.

18 *So Mary ... went and told the disciples ...* It is the familiar theme. Sight leads to insight, insight to belief, belief to witness.

Appearances to the disciples

19 *In the evening of that same day.* (v. 1.) This is the Roman demarcation of time to which gentile readers would be accustomed, not the Jewish system (19:14, 31).
The doors were closed ... Jesus came and stood among them. The body of the Risen Lord was unhindered by physical barriers, and he could be visible or not as he pleased (Lk 24:31, 36).
Peace be with you. (14:27.) His peace is his own special gift arising from his presence (vv. 21, 26; Lk 24:36).

20 *(He) showed them his hands and his side.* Although physical barriers now presented no obstacle, his body was the very same that had hung on the cross, marked for ever (Lk 24:39–40).
The disciples were filled with joy. (16:20.) As with Mary of Magdala there is joy and acceptance and no mention of fear.

21 *As the Father sent me, so am I sending you.* The disciples were thus commissioned by Jesus to carry out his work in the world as fully representative of him (17:18). Their primary task was to bear witness to the resurrection because they had been with him 'from the beginning'. Evidence in the New Testament supports the view that the apostles exercised authority over the Church (I Corinthians 12:27–28).

22 *He breathed on them.* It was the act of creation by which, through the gift of the Holy Spirit, the apostles became the Church, the body of Christ (2:21; 6:51–56). At the creation 'Yahweh God fashioned man of dust from the soil. Then he breathed into his nostrils a breath of life, and thus man became a living being' (Genesis 2:7). This is the beginning of a second creation as men receive

the life born of the Spirit (9:6–7). Luke uses a different tradition but it embodies the same teaching (Acts 2:1–13).

23 *Whose sins you forgive, they are forgiven.* (Mt 16:19; 18:18.) Sin is disobedience to the will of the Father, recognised as such by the individual conscience. It is on the authority of this saying that priests at their ordination are empowered to pronounce absolution as deputies of God. The knowledge that God forgives the really penitent is not always enough to remove the sense of guilt. Protestant sections of the Church maintain that all believers share in the priesthood and therefore in the authority to convey forgiveness.

24 *Thomas, called the Twin.* (11:16; 14:5.)

25 *Unless I see the holes . . . I refuse to believe.* It was the natural reaction to the news that Jesus had risen from the dead. Thomas represents the common sense of humanity throughout the ages.

26 *Eight days later.* On the following Sunday according to the Jewish reckoning (v. 1).

27 (*Jesus*) *spoke to Thomas.* Jesus knew about Thomas's refusal to believe though no one had been aware of his presence, and now he came specially on Thomas's account.

28 *My Lord and my God.* Confronted with the Risen Lord himself, worship was the only possible response. There was no need of verification. This confession of faith in Jesus as Lord and God is the climax to which the whole gospel has been leading.

29 *You believe because you can see me.* To see Jesus after the resurrection, to look at his wounds, to hear him talk, and even eat with him, was necessary if the

apostles were to witness to the actuality of the resurrection (Acts 10:40–41). When his appearances ceased, they had served their purpose.

Happy are those who have not seen and yet believe. The evidence of the senses ceased to be necessary because the Holy Spirit in and with believers, guides them and teaches them.

CONCLUSION

31 *These are recorded so that you may believe.* (1:12.)
Life through his name (3:5; 4:14; 6:53–54; 14:23; 15:4–5.)

APPENDIX

Chapters 1–20 are a clear literary unit rounded off with a fine conclusion at 20:31. The reason for adding another chapter has been much discussed but no common conclusion has been reached. There is nothing in either the language or style to rule out a single authorship of the whole work, and all existing manuscripts of the gospel, except one, include this chapter. There was a synoptic tradition about appearances in Galilee (Mt 28:10, 16–20; Mk 16:7) and John has perhaps drawn on this for the story of the miraculous catch which has points in common with Luke's account of the call of Peter (Lk 5:1–11). He seems to have used the story of an appearance of Jesus as a parable about the experience of disciples in the post-resurrection Church, and it will be noticed that some of the details are not consistent with what has been related in ch. 20. The account of Peter's reconciliation with Jesus is in this gospel only.

The appearance on the shore of Tiberias

21:1 *The Sea of Tiberias.* The lake of Galilee (6:1). If the story is to be understood as having parabolic significance, it should be remembered that the sea (6:17–21) represented the hostile world (17:18).

2 *Nathanael from Cana.* (1:45–51.)
The sons of Zebedee. James and John are often so described in the synoptic gospels, but this is the only place in Jn where they are mentioned at all. If John was the disciple Jesus loved, the opportunity to identify him as such was not taken (v. 7).

3 *I'm going fishing.* 'Fishing' is the synoptic metaphor for bringing men to Christ (Mt 4:19; Mk 1:17; Lk 5:10), and 'the world' (v. 1) was the sphere of the apostles' activity.
They ... caught nothing that night. Night was the best time for fishing but on their own they could accomplish nothing.

4 *There stood Jesus on the shore.* The fact that the disciples did not recognise him is difficult here because of the two earlier appearances in Jerusalem (20:19–29), but that ceases to be important if John is primarily intending to teach that Jesus meets his disciples in their ordinary occupations.

6 *They dropped the net ... they could not haul it in.* Under the direction of Jesus great things can be accomplished. It is interesting that the Greek word for 'haul' is the same as that used for 'draw' at 6:44, 'No one can come to me except the Father draw him'. The size of the catch recalls the abounding generosity at Cana (2:1–11), and the twelve hampers of scraps left over after the feeding of the five thousand.

7 *The disciple Jesus loved said. ... 'It is the Lord'.* Again he was the first to understand (20:5).
Simon Peter ... wrapped his cloak about him. As

before, Simon was the first to act. He could not
greet the Lord half-clad so he tucked up his cloak
and waded ashore.

9 *Bread . . . and . . . fish.* These were the symbols of the
Eucharist in the early Church (6:9). In the post-
resurrection era disciples withdraw from their
labours in 'the world' (v. 1) to meet Jesus at the
Eucharist.

10 *Bring some of the fish you have just caught.* Fish was
already cooking and more would seem to be unneces-
sary, but the great haul was Christ's gift and it was
right to bring him some in gratitude.

11 *Big fish, one hundred and fifty-three of them.* The
original meaning behind this precise figure has been
lost. Possibly it was believed that there was that
number of different species of fish and the inclusive-
ness of the Church's mission is thus suggested.
The net was unbroken. The undivided Church can
hold all who are drawn into it (10:16).

13 *Jesus . . . took the bread and gave it to them.* These
are the actions of the Eucharist (6:11). In the new
age which began with the resurrection the disciples
are sustained by the food Christ gives.

14 *This was the third time that Jesus showed himself.* In
ch. 20 there is the appearance to Mary of Magdala
as well as two appearances to the disciples (v. 4).

15 *After the meal.* The second part of the chapter is
concerned with Simon Peter and the disciple Jesus
loved. It may have been intended as an authoritative
statement to silence disputes between rival sup-
porters of the two apostles at Ephesus, or wherever
the gospel originated.
Simon . . . do you love me more than these others do?
Simon had compared himself with the others to their

218

disadvantage. They might run away at the moment
of crisis, but he never would (Mt 26:33; Mk 14:29).
Yes Lord, you know I love you. Simon evaded the
question. To deny the Lord was probably worse
than to desert him, and he saw that to measure his
worth against the brethren was wrong.
Feed my lambs. Peter had faced the truth about himself and could therefore be of service. He was
commissioned as a shepherd of the flock.

16 *A second time he said to him* ... The question of
comparison is dropped. All that matters is whether
Simon himself is totally committed to Christ.
Look after my sheep. The Lord does not wait for his
disciples to be entirely satisfactory before he uses
them. The commission is repeated.

17 *He said to him the third time* ... Simon was being
made to reverse his three denials, and forced to the
recognition that Jesus knew him better than he knew
himself. Humility and trust are the characteristics of
true discipleship.
Feed my sheep. Simon was qualified for the work
allotted to him.

18 *You will stretch out your hands.* It was a prediction
of Peter's crucifixion (13:36).
Somebody ... will put a belt round you. Victims were
fastened in position by ropes.

19 *He indicated the kind of death by which Peter would
give glory to God.* Peter was martyred, so bearing
witness to the truth (1:19-51). The witness of the
Baptist came to full fruition in the mature disciples
of the post-resurrection Church.
Follow me. Readiness to die for Christ is implied in
the command (Mk 8:34).

22 *If I want him to stay behind till I come* ... If it was
the Lord's will that he should live until the Second

Coming then that was where his vocation as a
disciple lay. It was not Peter's business.

23 *The rumour went out . . . that this disciple would not
die.* It was important that the rumour should be
countered. Jesus had made no pronouncement about
the time of his death, and according to tradition he
lived to a great age (Introduction A.).

24 *This disciple.* The disciple Jesus loved vouches for
the truth of the gospel. He has transmitted the truth
through his writing and is just as much of a witness
as Peter, though of a different kind.
We know that his testimony is true. Elders of the
Church at Ephesus perhaps, or a group of John's
disciples, answer for the truth of what is contained
in the book (15:27; 19:35).